CHAKA BOOKER

THE POWER
YOU HAVE TO
LAND THE JOB
THE YOU DESERVE
EMPOWERED
CANDIDATE

Published by Westgate Media
Copy Editor: Rebecca Nutting
Cover Design: Sev Sukander
Interior Design: Booknook.biz

ISBN 978-1-7349048-0-2 (ePUB)
ISBN 978-1-7349048-2-6 (MOBI)
ISBN 978-1-7349048-1-9 (Print)

Library of Congress Control Number: 2020906803
Printed in the United States of America
10 9 8 7 6 5 4 3 2 1

CONTENTS

INTRODUCTION

The Odds

In order to land a job, at some point you'll find yourself sitting across from an interviewer as they pepper you with questions. Those are pivotal moments which determine whether you land the job. Given the importance of those interactions, what do you suppose the odds are that the person across the table will make the right hiring decision?

Frank L. Schmidt, a psychologist renowned for his research in personnel selection, had the same question. To find the answer, he partnered with John E. Hunter, a psychologist with deep expertise in research methodology. Together, they conducted a meta-analysis on eighty-five years of research on interviews.[1] The results were far from encouraging.

When you sit at that interview table, the odds of the right decision* being made are 54 percent.

That's right. Fifty-four percent.

And that was the high end. Schmidt and Hunter analyzed nearly twenty different methods for assessing talent, some of which only had 38 percent accuracy. They also experimented with various combinations of assessment types (work samples, knowledge tests, etc.) but only managed to nudge results slightly past 60 percent.

Other researchers have since tackled the same question, with similar results. Depending on the position you are applying for—it can actually get worse. A Gallup study discovered

---

* A "right" decision was measured on two scales commonly used in personnel research. The math is complex, but simply put, they measured the dollar value of an employee's output and their output as a percentage of the average output.

that as high as *82 percent* of management interviews lead to the *wrong* hiring decision.[2]

In the US alone, there are 6 million small business owners with employees, 5 million HR and recruitment professionals, 2 million general managers and 238 thousand CEOs. That doesn't include the countless co-workers and team members who are asked every day to help interview candidates for positions on their teams.

For most of them, interviewing isn't a part of their job. Most them have not had the opportunity to develop into strong interviewers. *The majority of them are average interviewers.*

That's not an insult, it's just a reality of the hiring process. The dismal odds exist for a simple reason—most people don't interview often enough to be great at it. They interview just enough to be average. Fifty percent is average. With those odds, interviewers would be better off simply tossing a coin. They'd save everyone valuable time and get the same results. As a candidate, that's bad news.

The good news is you can dramatically beat those odds.

Landing your next job doesn't have to be a coin toss.

The reason I know this is because I'm the interviewer on the other side of the table.

The Other Side of the Table

Shortly after graduating from Stanford University with an MBA, I began working for one of the richest men in America—billionaire Eli Broad. He is the founder of two Fortune 500 companies: KB Home and SunAmerica. He's also the philanthropist behind the Broad Museum in Los Angeles, the Broad Institute of MIT and Harvard, the Eli Broad College of Business in Michigan, and multiple other institutions.

He had recently launched his newest venture, the Broad Center—which recruits and trains professionals from across the country for leadership positions in the public sector—and needed someone to help find talented people with the skill and will to do tough, gritty work. That someone was me.

I started my career with the center as a recruiter. I eventually led the recruitment team and then became a managing director. I've since spent more than the fifteen years assessing and developing talent from a wide range of industries and have interviewed candidates, from Fortune 500s, to start-ups, and everything in between. I've assessed professionals who went to top universities and those who didn't. Consulting, marketing, finance, education, operations, military, technology, engineering—you name it, I've interviewed someone with that background.

Along the way, I've been fortunate to co-interview alongside professionals with experience in a range of high-performing organizations—IBM, Goldman Sachs, McKinsey, Google. Each of them with expertise that has shaped my understanding of how to effectively assess talent.

The lessons I learned are captured in my first book, *Mastering the Hire: 12 Strategies to Improve Your Odds of Making the Right Hire*. That book was written for interviewers—the people doing the hiring—not for candidates. It draws on over a decade of first-hand experience, as well as data and research from the fields of psychology, cognitive science, and behavioral economics.

I wrote that book for the same reason I wrote this book, to increase the odds of people landing the job they deserve. In order to do that, we need to rethink what an interview truly is.

The Definition

So, what is an interview? It seems like a simple question. Everyone believes they know the answer. That's why it's important to start there. Let's look at several common definitions.

- *Merriam-Webster:* n. a formal consultation usually to evaluate qualifications (as of a prospective student or employee)
- *Cambridge Dictionary:* n. a formal meeting at which a person who is interested in getting a job or other position is asked questions to learn how well the person would be able to do it
- *Oxford Dictionary:* v. to question (someone) to discover their opinions or experience • to orally examine (an applicant for a job, college admission, etc.)

At first glance, nothing seems out of place. These definitions are what you'd expect to find when describing an interview. But they could just as easily be written as:

- *Merriam-Webster:* n. a formal consultation usually to share one's qualifications (e.g., to a prospective employer interested in hiring someone talented)
- *Cambridge Dictionary:* n. a formal meeting in which a person who is interested in a job has the opportunity to share how well they would be able to do it
- *Oxford Dictionary:* v. to provide one's opinions or experience • to verbally express oneself

The shift is subtle, but important. The first set of definitions, the ones you'll find in any dictionary, are from the perspective of the interviewer. The second set are written from the perspective of the candidate. The candidate-centered definition doesn't represent a significant change in the meaning of the word "interview" and could be used in any dictionary.

But you won't find it in any dictionary.

Why not? Could it be that Merriam-Webster, Cambridge, and Oxford are part of a worldwide conspiracy to disempower candidates? Has every editor at every publisher of dictionaries somehow made the exact same mistake?

No, there isn't a conspiracy. The choice to focus on one definition over the other isn't intentional. But the *lack* of intention is what's *most* damaging about the definition. The definitions are all written from the interviewer's perspective because of a belief we've been taught to accept without question—that the interviewer is in control of the interview.

That belief is false.

The Truth

At first glance, the belief that the interviewer is in control seems logical. Since the interviewer controls the hiring decision, they must also control the interview. While the first half of that belief is accurate, the second half represents an error in thinking that puts every candidate at a disadvantage. That assumption automatically disempowers you and impacts your belief in what else is possible.

To find the truth about who is in control, we need to put modern definitions aside and look to the original meaning of the word from the sixteenth century. The Middle French origin of "interview" is:

Entrevue: derived from "*s'entrevoir*," to see each other, visit each other briefly, have a glimpse of

This definition is untainted by the present-day experience of job interviewing and provides greater insight. An interview is people spending time together—a visit. It is not a one-sided event in which the interviewer has all the power and control. It is an interaction. Each side seeing and influencing each other along the way.

This definition holds true today and gives us an understanding of what truly happens at the interview table. During an interview, the power is shared. If you've ever prepared for an interview—researched the role, rehearsed answers, brushed up your resume, etc.—you intuitively already know you have some control.

But how much *more* power could you have?

That's a hard question for any candidate to answer. On average, people switch employers every 4.3 years (for those aged twenty-five to thirty-four, it's 2.8 years).[3] In other words, candidates only interview every three to four years. They don't interview enough to see patterns that reveal what they can and can't control.

My experience has been the opposite. I've interviewed more than three thousand candidates from every corner of the country. I've seen candidates succeed. I've seen them fail. I've witnessed the differences in what they do. Being so close to talent day in and day out has allowed me to see the patterns. It has forced me to reexamine what happens during an interview. I've learned that the belief about who has power and control is based on the misperception that during an interview, the interviewer is assessing the candidate.

You are likely asking yourself, "Wait, the interviewer is *not* assessing the candidate?" This misperception is so integral to the definition of an interview that other explanations don't seem plausible. It's confusing. So, let's spend a moment thinking about what happens during an interview.

Who's Assessing What?

During an interview, the interviewer is the person asking the questions. So far so good. But when you analyze what happens next, the belief about who is in control falls apart. The first thing the candidate does in response to a question is dive into their memory bank and select from a range of experiences, perspectives, and opinions. When they come back out, they share what they found. The interviewer then asks them what they did well, what they could have done better, and what they would do differently next time.

When you tilt the interview to look at it from this angle, you realize the interviewer isn't actually assessing the candidate. What the interviewer has just done is ask the candidate to retrieve a memory and assess it themselves. The interviewer is judging the quality and relevance of the candidate's *self-assessment*. They are assessing what the candidate has *chosen* to share.

From this perspective, you begin to realize how much power the candidate has. In nearly every moment of the interview process, the hiring organization is dependent on you to provide information they need. The resume you submit is created by you. During the interview, you control which memories to share. You control what you want to say about those experiences. You control the answers you prepare in advance. After the interview, you control who to provide as references.

Across my career I've reflected on every interview I've conducted. I've analyzed every mistake, questioned every belief, refined, experimented, studied, documented, and reflected again. While it is true that the interviewer ultimately makes the final decision, I can say with certainty that the candidate who understands the process of interviewing and the mechanics of decision-making—has far more power over that decision than they realize.

This book is about understanding the power you have and using it to land the job you deserve.

THE ELEVEN POWERS

The fact that interviews often misidentify talent means if you leave all the power in the interviewer's hands, you won't get the job. At best, you'll have the same odds as anyone else. But if you realize the power you have and how to use it, your chances of landing the job you deserve will dramatically increase.

Candidates often approach the hiring process thinking primarily about themselves. They enter the interview with a set of answers they've practiced for questions they may or may not be asked. That preparation is important, but it's tactical. It's what everyone does. To advance in the hiring process, it will take more than a set of prepared answers.

To succeed, you must also examine everything through the lens of the interviewer. Understanding the person on the other side of the table and the multiple dynamics shaping the final decision will put you in control. To beat the odds, you need strategies with specific practices that you can easily grasp and consistently execute.

This book provides eleven strategies, each with specific practices that give you power and control during the interview. It is split into four sections, each containing specific areas of power. Section One is about the work you've done, your experiences, and the optimal ways to frame and communicate that information. Section Two is about the mind of the interviewer and how to best navigate the way people think so they accurately see your talent. In Section Three, the lens is turned inward and focuses on maximizing your nonverbal signals, emotions, and thought processes. Section Four provides unique approaches to using time, sleep, and practice to boost the performance needed to succeed in an arena designed for everyone to fail—except one. The book closes with two chapters that provide specific insight on landing a job during a crisis, a time when hiring decisions and the future are both uncertain.

As you read through the book, you'll be tempted to figure out how to use *all* of it in your next interview. Don't take that approach. It will leave you overwhelmed because it isn't the way to use a book like this. There are too many practices to effectively understand and execute at the level needed to shift the odds in your favor. In addition, not all the approaches will suit your personality, background, or even beliefs. The better approach is to tailor this book to who you are and what you are trying to accomplish.

Customize the Eleven Powers

When it comes to expressing who you are and what you can do, there is no one-size-fits-all strategy. You do not want to force any of these tactics into your communication style, approach to relationship-building, identity, or circumstances. Instead, you want to customize the strategies. Begin by reading the book, and within each section, note the strategies that most interest you. Make sure to also note those that will push you a little out of your comfort zone. Exploring that discomfort, coupled with practice, is time well spent because it is often where you can most dramatically shift the odds.

Don't practice any strategies as you are reading. Just work your way through the book and take note of anything that feels like it could work for you. When you are done with the book, jot into a separate document all the strategies that you flagged. Keep them separated by category so you know the context in which they operate. Now, scan the list.

You may find that some of the practices overlap, maybe even conflict, because they can be applied during the same part of the interview process. For example, throughout the book, you will find preparation strategies that are implemented just before the start of the interview. Executing all of them isn't the goal. It's unlikely that you'll do breathing exercises, a practice based on laughter, cognitive reframing, and body language adjustments—all in combination shortly before the interview.

Context and Time
Instead, when practices overlap or conflict, determine which outcomes are most important for your context, or best fit your style and comfort level. Then pick the practices that match your specific circumstances. To be successful, your *context* has to drive your strategy. Sometimes, however, *time* has to drive your strategy. You may find yourself in a situation where you don't have time to learn a wide range of interviewing techniques. In that case, determine which ones you are most comfortable implementing, and eliminate the ones you are less comfortable with. When you do have time, push yourself to explore the one that allows you to grow even more and reach even higher levels of performance.

Whenever I help people prepare for interviews, I'm able to get to know them and their context. That is impossible to do through a book. There is no way for me to prioritize these strategies without knowing you and your context. Everything advised in this book will work. Having spent many years on the interviewer's side, I've learned how easily I can be at the mercy of the candidate if they understand how my mind works and the way the system is built.

How to combine the strategies depends entirely on the knowledge that only you hold—who you are, and the environment you will be operating in. I am confident in these strategies and equally confident that you can build a personalized strategy that helps you succeed during your next interview.

Unforced Errors

An interview is a mechanism for identifying whether a candidate is best for the job. That statement, although true, anchors heavily on what happens by the end of the hiring process. When the process is over, the interviewer hopes to have found the best candidate. But *during* the interview process, a significant portion of the decision-making is driven by something other than finding the best candidate.

It is driven by the interviewer's desire to not pick the worst candidate.

This occurs because interviewers tend to be risk-averse and evaluating another person's potential is a complex task. Interviews require the interviewer to use a set of criteria to assess a range of characteristics the candidate may or may not exhibit during an in-the-moment experience that evolves with each question.

Our brains, which prefer to process information efficiently, attack this complexity by finding ways to simplify the decision. During an interview, it is easier to find mistakes or spot missteps the candidate makes. The interviewer's mind latches onto this efficiency and the process of finding the best candidate becomes the simpler task of eliminating candidates who prove they aren't the best. The interesting thing to note is that candidates don't just eliminate themselves by committing errors, they do so by committing *unforced errors*.

A Tennis Lesson

In the game of tennis, there are two types of errors—forced errors and unforced errors. Forced errors occur when a player hits a shot strong enough or well-placed enough that their opponent can't return it. An unforced error is an error a player makes that wasn't created by their opponent. For example, an unforced error is when a tennis player serves their own ball into the net or outside the lines. That ball was in their control and they missed a point due to their own misjudgment or action.

A study by the *British Journal of Sports Medicine* found that the average tennis player loses many more points due to unforced errors than due to winning shots by their opponent. The study found that if the rate of unforced errors can be reduced, it would increase the odds of winning. This was echoed decades earlier by famous tennis champion Bill Tilden who once commented, "Matches are always lost on errors and never won by placements." Strong players may consistently place the ball better, but a significant part of their success is they don't beat themselves.

Eliminate Unforced Errors
The power of unforced errors to influence outcomes is found across all activities in which performance is being measured, including interviewing. I've consistently witnessed strong candidates commit unforced errors and eventually get dropped from consideration. As the competition gets tighter, unforced errors become even more damaging because all the candidates are strong. At those later stages of the hiring process, it gets harder for interviewers to separate one strong candidate from another and errors end up winnowing the pool.

As the candidate, this is an opportunity to take back control. Identifying, controlling, and minimizing every possible unforced error is fundamental to succeeding during a hiring process. Many of the strategies and techniques in this book are about reducing unforced errors. For example, not custom-building your resume, not knowing the optimal length of an answer, and practicing incorrectly are all examples of unforced errors. The interviewer has nothing to do with whether those occur or not. You have complete power to either commit the error or eliminate it.

Throughout the book, I'll indicate unforced errors. These are often the mistakes you assume you won't make. As a result, some of the advice provided may seem commonplace. It will be important to take note of those errors because the assumption that you won't make them is part of the reason why you will. At a minimum, understand the research behind them and then eliminate every one of them from your next interview. You'll gain a significant edge over candidates who aren't empowered with the knowledge of how to avoid them.

Who You Are and the Life You Want

There is more to this book than just getting a job. Interviewing is a means for bringing you a step closer to the life you want. But if you aren't careful, you can lose who you are along the way. As you work through this book, you may feel the tension of portraying yourself as someone you aren't.

Treat those moments with the respect they deserve. Explore them and trust your instinct. The idea that you shouldn't stray too far from who you truly are isn't just core to this book, it is core to your success in life.

Attempting to be someone you are not is a concept that has been studied for more than two thousand years. Cicero, the Roman philosopher who took a stand against Julius Caesar, wrote a treatise in 44 BC called *On Duties*. Although its central theme is on how to live a good life, it could have been written for the modern-day job candidate. Cicero shared that we must "follow the bent of our own particular nature and even if other careers should be better and nobler, we may still regulate our own pursuits by the standard of our own nature." He continues to explain that it is a waste of time to fight against one's nature and to do so "is in direct opposition to one's natural genius."

Not every job you pursue will perfectly align with your genius. That's normal and to be expected. But straying too far from who you are, just for a job, can lead you to become someone you don't want to be. You should seek work that pushes you toward both financial success and personal fulfillment. This book is intended for you to do both. During an interview, you can both persuade and stay true to yourself. Finding that balance isn't easy, but for more than two thousand years, that has been the path that leads to success and happiness on multiple levels.

That isn't meant to be an idealistic pitch on identifying your dream job or finding your passion. That may not be your current reality. You may be thinking, "I just need a job, I've got bills to pay." I've been in those shoes, but in that case, you need a job from which you won't get fired within six months.

It is important you identify work you are good at, and that will provide some level of satisfaction. If you get a job that you can't do well, you'll soon find yourself out of work and interviewing again. Each time that happens, you'll have to create a story to explain your short stint to the next employer. Getting hired will keep getting harder. On the other hand, your job will take up two-thirds of your waking hours and unless you find some satisfaction in it, you will be miserable. Misery leads either to quitting, or staying and living with regrets. None of those are the life you want.

The point of becoming empowered during an interview is to land the job you deserve—which is a job you like and can do well, and that will build toward the future you've envisioned for yourself. If you find a job that meets those criteria, you won't just be able to pay the bills today, you'll have work that provides fulfillment across many years.

Authenticity and Honesty
Central to the balance needed for success are the ideals of authenticity and honesty. This book isn't about changing who

you are or deceiving interviewers. Some of the approaches may not be the way you would normally communicate or approach a conversation. But it's important to remember, an interview isn't a normal conversation. It is an attempt by someone who doesn't know you—to get to know you. At the end of the interview, they will think they know you—whether they truly do or not.

The power you have to help them understand who you are cannot hinge solely on you being authentic. Although authenticity is important, it is only one part of the equation. Equally important is how the interviewer *interprets* what they discover about you. You can't risk leaving that interpretation in their hands. You must learn how to control their discovery process, which means you may have to express yourself differently than you normally would.

Be careful not to think of strategies that give you power and control as ways to trick the interviewer into giving you a job. That view is extremely short-sighted. As a friend once told me, "Lying during an interview might get you the job, but it won't get you far." A report by ADP Screening and Selection Services discovered that in 2.6 million background checks, 41 percent of candidates lied about their education and 44 percent lied about their work experience.[4] That is not the path you want to take.

If you don't have the skills an interviewer asks for, but you lie and say you do, you are setting yourself up for failure because you will struggle with the job. Acknowledging that you have a deficit, but are a fast learner, is the better approach and far different than saying "Yes, I've done that." Your job is to persuade and convince the interviewer. Lying is neither persuading nor convincing. It is deceiving. Not only is it dishonorable, research has shown it to be a horrible strategy.

A study[5] conducted by psychologists from the University of California, Santa Barbara; and Texas Christian University focused on the "accuracy of deception judgments." In other words, they wanted to find out if people knew when other people were lying. Their study synthesized research from over twenty-four thousand people and found the odds of someone knowing when you aren't telling the truth are 54 percent. Once again, we find ourselves at the mercy of a coin toss. If you lie during an interview, you only have a fifty-fifty chance of getting away with it. Those aren't the odds you want in an interview. Every strategy in this book is designed to push your odds much higher. Don't send those odds backward by losing your integrity.

What you must accomplish during an interview is being authentic about who you are, truthful about what you can do, and incredibly strategic about how you present those things.

That is what this book will empower you to do. Let's begin.

SECTION ONE

The optimal ways to frame and communicate your experience, skills, and the work you've done.

CONTROLLING INFORMATION

One of the most renowned experts in the field of persuasion was Wayne C. Booth, a professor from the University of Chicago. Booth dedicated his life to studying the art of persuasion and in 1963, coined the term "rhetorical stance." The term is widely used by those who study influence and is also referred to as your "position" or your "footing" during an argument.

An argument is like a fight. It is verbal sparring between two people on opposite sides of an issue. As any fighter knows, if your stance—your footing—isn't correct, you will be at a disadvantage. Fortunately, during an interview you are neither fighting nor arguing. You are, however, trying to persuade them of something they aren't sure of yet, which is that you are the best fit for the job. While you and the interviewer may not be on opposite sides, you are looking at this decision from different angles. To succeed you need to understand the concept of footing. Booth once said:

> "In short, when you talk, you adjust your rhetorical stance continually, using different techniques for different people in various situations."

During your interviews, you will be in front of various people in various situations. Your position is that you are the right person to hire. What footing will best help make that argument? Those who study persuasion point to four strategies that give you power when making a point:

- Facts
- Definition/Redefinition
- Quality
- Relevance

If you translate this into the context of an interview, when you are asked a question, your answer will be based on one of the following strategies:

- If you have facts—strong examples that demonstrate your relevant skills and experience with the subject of the question—then use them.
- When you don't have facts, then redefine the question and discuss something else in your experience that is of equal or higher quality.
- Finally, establish that this other area is relevant.[*]

These strategies leverage the power of intelligently controlling information and are the basis of what you'll learn in this chapter. This is not about mistruths. You will be sharing facts. You won't take credit for things you didn't do or make claims that

---

[*] In the traditional definition of rhetoric, establishing relevance requires you to claim the interviewer's question is irrelevant. That wouldn't serve you well during an interview. We'll adjust that strategy and instead focus on the most relevant things to share, regardless of the job you are applying for.

can't be supported. Controlling truthful information is a better strategy than creating lies that need to be remembered.

The facts are about you, what you've accomplished, where you've succeeded, and where you've failed. The facts are yours. There is absolutely no reason you shouldn't control what the interviewer knows about you. Everything from the resume to the final reference check—comes from you. That footing is what controlling information is all about. In abstract, this may seem complicated. But it is straightforward, and it all starts with your resume.

HOW YOUR RESUME GIVES YOU POWER

When you do research about how to find a job, you'll find experts who suggest submitting resumes for jobs is an increasingly irrelevant approach. Instead, they recommend networking with the right people, joining professional groups relevant to your industry, cleaning up your social media, and a range of other activities.

That is great advice for getting a foot in the door to get an interview. But this book isn't about *getting* an interview. It's about what to do *during* the interview. During the interview, your resume is incredibly important because it is a source of information that will influence what the interviewer thinks about you. It contains the facts you choose to share and is the footing that influences their initial opinion.

The paradox about resumes is that interviewers often spend very little time on them. Until recently, research found interviewers spent four to five minutes reviewing a resume. But in 2018, a study[0] using eye-tracking software was conducted to more accurately determine how long interviewers look at resumes. Their research showed that, on average, interviewers initially review a resume for only 7.4 seconds.

That may seem like a very short amount of time to make a decision about a candidate. But keep in mind they aren't making a deep, evaluative decision during that first scan. They are just deciding if they should invest more time in getting to know you. If they make that initial decision in your favor, they will revisit the resume the day of the interview. It is during that second review that your resume will receive more attention, which is where the original research on the four to five minutes came from.

I've seen this play out three ways. Some interviewers quickly scan your resume when they first receive it. Then shortly before the interview, they spend another five minutes reviewing it. During this review, they jot down their reactions and prep off-the-cuff interview questions to ask. Other interviewers do the same thing, but they are more thorough. This second type of interviewer also quickly scans your resume when they first receive it. But before the interview, they spend far more time on the resume taking detailed notes. The third type of interviewer is at the other end of the spectrum. While they may have briefly seen it beforehand, they will mainly review your resume *while* they are interviewing you. They may have stock questions they've been assigned to ask you, and simultaneously, they'll generate questions in the moment based on what they are reading about you.

Hook and Shape: The Dual Power of Your Resume

While it may be discouraging to see the depth of preparation falls across such a wide range, what is most important is that every one of those interviewers is influenced by the piece of paper in front of them. Either because they didn't spend much time and are taking it at face value, or because they dug deep and have specific areas of interest based on what they read. What occurs during those distinct moments when your resume is in front of the interviewer drives the dual purpose of the resume.

First, it is the hook that makes the interviewer put your resume in the "advance" pile. Second, once you are in the room with the interviewer, the resume defines what they think about you. These two interactions with your resume highlight the power of using it to strategically drive the conversations you will eventually have. Since you decide what is written on that piece of paper, you are the one who establishes the facts that will drive some of the questions they will ask you.

That is powerful footing and you must take advantage of it by custom-building your resume for each job you want. Tailoring your resume is the foundation for the strategies in this chapter. Fortunately, that doesn't mean you need to start from scratch. Instead, start with your current resume as the base.

The Base Resume and LinkedIn

Your base resume is similar to the version you should have on LinkedIn. You can't customize your LinkedIn profile for each job. So, your online profile needs to include your education, key skills, experiences, accomplishments, awards, affiliations, and words targeted to your *industry*. If you are switching industries, then scrub words or jargon that won't be understood outside your industry. If you are trying to switch roles (e.g., from operations to marketing), then don't spend too much time to generalize your actual work experience; that will result in it seeming generic. Instead, use the LinkedIn "About" section as the place to strategically describe yourself. That space, situated near the top of your profile, is perfect to shape how the rest of your description will be perceived by describing skills and experiences that are valuable regardless of the role.[*]

Custom-Build Your Resume

The base resume, whether on paper or LinkedIn, is your starting point. The next step is to visit the website for the job you are pursuing and pull relevant keywords or descriptors to capture specific areas around which you'll customize your resume.

You likely have heard of this approach, particularly in the context of resume-screening algorithms and artificial intelligence that organizations are increasingly using. Because some

---

[*] This book won't go into detail on creating a strong LinkedIn profile. There is great insight easily found on the topic through an online search.

job postings attract a high volume of resumes, it can be imprac-
tical for companies to have a human scanning each one as it
arrives. Instead, they use software that searches the resume for
phrases, keywords, and relevant text that align with the criteria
for the ideal candidate. Depending on the software, organizations can determine which keywords should be prioritized and
how they should be scored.

The important thing to recognize is that artificial intelligence and algorithms are built to do what the human mind does.
In other words, customizing your resume doesn't only help you
get past potential resume-screening software, it helps you connect with the people who will eventually look at your resume.

There are three areas specific to the role and organization
that you want to use for tailoring your resume. These areas
are shared below, beginning with those that are more directly
observable and therefore more easily found, and ending with
areas that other candidates are likely not considering because
they aren't surface level. This same order is also what moves
you from simply creating a resume that beats algorithms to one
that engages the human minds that will determine if you can
beat other candidates.

Skills

The first area in which you'll custom-build relevancy are
skills you'll need for the job. The place to find those are in the
"Qualifications" section and the "Responsibilities" section of
the job description. Look for the desired skills and cross-refer-
ence them with the bullets in your base resume that indicate
work similar to those keywords. If your bullet doesn't contain
the relevant word, then rewrite the bullet to include the word. If
you've done work that reflects a keyword, but haven't included
it as a bullet, then write a new bullet including the work and
that specific word.

Fit

Using words from the Qualifications and Responsibilities sections serves to positively trigger the logical conclusion that you have relevant skills. There is, however, another angle for which the resume is helpful—the emotional angle.* When interviewers are reviewing your resume, they aren't just looking to see if you can do the job, they are also beginning to answer the question, "Will this person fit in here?" That is a question most interviewers consciously begin to think about during the interview. Successful candidates begin planting that seed far earlier, with their resume.

To do this, find the page on their website about their organization's core values and beliefs. Another place to find this language is by searching for videos or articles featuring the CEO or other leaders in the organization. Senior leaders love talking about culture and values. In that language, you will find words that the interviewer is accustomed to hearing about how they and their teams should operate.

Identify those words that identify their values, beliefs, and culture, and determine which ones align with your own values and beliefs. Then, include those words throughout your resume as well. Using both logic and emotion keeps your content relevant and will speak much more directly to the interviewer.†

The "How"

Many candidates are aware of aligning their resume and interview answers with the employer's desired skills. Thinking about the above-mentioned fit at the resume stage puts you

---

* The strategies of using logic and emotion are important and later chapters will discuss them both.

† In Section 2 we will return to the "power of familiarity" and how to use it during the interview.

a notch ahead of most. But there is one more area that most candidates overlook when preparing that will put you even further in the lead. When interviewers are assessing talent, they aren't just interested in the candidate's skills and fit with their organization's culture, they also want to know how they do the work they do.

When you use the job description as your preparation guide—don't just look for *what* they want you to do, but also *how* they want you to do it. The desired skills are generally easier to spot. Identifying the "how" can be more complicated. It often isn't called out individually. To separate the two, think of skills as something you could learn in a class or course. Think of the "how" as soft skills. They are often more about your personality, the way people would describe you, the things shaped by your experiences that generally aren't taught in classes.

Below is an example of the responsibilities and qualifications of a project manager. After each line, I've written whether it indicates a "what" or a "how."

Project Manager – Job Description

Responsibilities
Schedule regular meetings and record decisions (*what*)
Create and maintain workflows (*what*)
Break projects into tasks with timeframes and goals (*what*)
Prepare documentation for internal teams and key stakeholders (*what*)
Track expenses and predict future costs (*what*)
Coordinate quality controls to ensure deliverables meet requirements (*what*)
Represent the company at conferences and events (*what*)
Measure and report on project performance (*what*)

Qualifications
Knowledge of project management software (*what*)
Flexible and comfortable with ambiguity (*how*)
Team spirit (*how*)
Excellent written and verbal communication skills (*what*)
Experience with confidential company information (*how*)
Ability to problem-solve (*what*)
Detail-oriented and efficient (*how*)
Bachelor's in Business Administration or related field (*what*)

Do this exercise with the job description as well as any preamble they include about the team or organization. Most candidates are prepared to talk about what they can do. But this exercise prepares you to demonstrate how you do what you do. Using the project manager example from above, this exercise informs you that they are looking for a person who:

Is good at adjusting when things change, has a personality that shows team spirit, knows how to operate with discretion, values details and efficiency.

Find ways to incorporate this into your resume and as you prepare potential answers to interview questions. This type of preparation gives you more control over the relevancy of your answers than most candidates, which is the edge you need in order to come out ahead.

Customizing Defines the Questions
The keywords you include are the ones the interviewer will be scanning for to make a quick decision about relevancy. But what you are also building is a resume that will make them ask the interview questions you want them to ask. I previously

described three different types of interviewers and the depth in which they review your resume. Their approach is sometimes driven by the organization's approach to using resumes during an interview. Some organizations believe in doing a thorough review of your resume during the interview. Other organizations will spend very little time discussing your resume with you, potentially dedicating only a portion of an interview specifically to it.

If they are an organization that does thorough resume reviews, they will take an entire interview and work through your resume in chronological order and ask you questions about each role and/or organization you've worked in. They will ask questions such as:

- "What did you accomplish in this role?"
- "What did you learn in this role?"
- "Did you achieve this goal as an individual or as a team?"
- "Why did you leave this role?"
- "Why did you take on this next role?"

If they don't do an entire interview focused on the resume, they will do the same as above, but only ask a few questions about some of your roles and then spend the rest of the time on traditional interview questions. You usually can't predict their approach. But if you custom-build your resume, you'll be thinking differently about how to create your resume, which allows you to be prepared either way.

Your Resume Is a Trailer
When the interviewer first sees your resume, reviewing it is just a task that they must do. You aren't a person to them yet, it is only a sheet of paper. But when structured correctly, your

resume gives you the power to make them interested to learn more and shapes the questions they will ask.

Think of your resume as a trailer for a movie about you. It is not intended to capture every single accomplishment you've achieved and every possible skill you've attained. It is designed to intrigue them with enough details to begin understanding what you are about. In doing so, it puts the story you want in their mind.

Since you are the one creating the trailer, you should include the elements you'll be prepared to speak about when asked. Custom-building your resume is a powerful way to control some of what the interviewer will ask you because it pushes them to ask questions you are ready to answer. To accomplish this, you should prepare to discuss the following for every bullet on your resume:

- Some context to explain your responsibilities.
- The results you accomplished.
- What you could have done better.

Some candidates struggle with determining the balance of responsibilities versus results to include on the resume. A rule of thumb to solve this is that the more years of experience you have, the more your accomplishments should outweigh responsibilities. If you are more junior, then focus more on the responsibilities than the accomplishments.

Although individual interviewers each have personal preferences for what they want in a resume, across all interviewers there are key structural elements that increase the odds of your resume advancing and generating questions you want to answer.

Formatting
When interviewers read a resume for the first time, they are scanning, searching for tidbits to make a decision as quickly as

possible. Later, they are looking for questions to ask. Your job is to help them do that. In other words, make it easy to review by keeping it well-organized and formatted.

The primary debate about how to format a resume is whether to structure it chronologically or functionally (i.e., if you've worked in marketing and operations and chose the functional format, your resume would have a "Marketing" section and an "Operations" section).

There really shouldn't be a debate. Structure it chronologically. Not only do the majority of interviewers prefer that format, study after study has found that our brains measure things in terms of time. In the words of famed neuroscientist Dean Buonomano, "Your brain is a time machine."[2] It is human nature to measure things chronologically. Don't fight nature and play the odds that are in your favor:

- Put your work experiences in order from most recent role to oldest role.
- Always include start and end dates, titles, and bullets with descriptors.

That format allows interviewers to easily see where you worked, how long you worked there, and what you did while you were there.

There is an argument for using a functional resume, but it runs counter to the principle of making a resume easy to read. Those who advise using a functional resume suggest using that format when you want to draw attention away from job hopping, employment gaps, a short career, or other factors that may be less attractive. The idea behind that strategy is that it obscures the truth. That is a short-sighted strategy, because the truth always comes to light. At some point, they will figure out whatever it is you are hiding, and it will become a problem.

Ultimately, it is your decision based on your context. But in my experience, I have never met an interviewer who preferred the functional resume.

Distraction-free
To help make the resume easy to read, be sure to make it free from distractions. Once again, the advice you'll find that works for artificial intelligence is relevant for human intelligence. When it comes to resume-scanning software, it's been found that they struggle with unique fonts, tables, images, etc. The same is true for interviewers. The following rarely add value to your resume and more commonly hurt your odds.

- *Photos*: Photos are always judged. Sometimes in your favor, sometimes not. Either way, they distract from what matters most—what you can do.
- *Fancy fonts*: Unless you're getting a job in which your artistic creativity is a necessary skill, keep it neutral. Stick with Times New Roman or Calibri fonts.
- *Bold fonts*: Do not bold anything other than your name, title, and organization. Making anything bold does draw the interviewer's eyes to specific items— but you don't know if that is where their eye should be drawn. They know what they are looking for; they don't need your help.
- *Images/clip art/graphics*: There are no images, clip art, or graphics that convey the message you want better than the words on the page—don't include them.

Doing any of the above will distract the interviewer. It opens the door to judgment about something other than what you've done. You want them to form an opinion of your work experience, not how you've chosen to document your work experience.

Include numbers

Whenever possible, include quantitative information about your accomplishments. If you increased sales by a certain percentage, reduced cost by a certain amount of dollars, improved efficiency by a certain measure, or anything similar—include the numbers.

By including numbers, you are giving them an easy reason to move you to the "advance" pile. Research has shown that including statistics and or any other quantitative representation of your accomplishments is important because it anchors your work in something that feels factual.[3] Numbers allow the interviewer to mentally check off a measure of whether you have accomplished tangible things.

The interviewer won't be fact-checking as they scan your resume, but don't fabricate numbers because when they meet you, they will ask about them. That is exactly what you want. The numbers will shape their questions and you'll be ready. But be careful not to overdo it. Don't include numbers with every line. That isn't convincing and works against you because it is too much to process and will slow them down.

The occasional presence of numbers provides a type of evidence that feels harder to refute. Numbers add weight to written words and make a subconscious argument that helps convince the interviewer of your accomplishments. That is exactly what you want in that moment. You want them to believe in you enough to want to learn more about a topic you're prepared to discuss.

Keep it short

Depending on the industry you are in, there will be different guidance for resume length. But in most cases, unless the interviewer is hiring for an academic role, they won't care how many papers you've written, how many speeches you've delivered, nor

17

do they need quotes from people who you've worked with. Multiple pages of supporting documents do very little if the first two pages don't hook the interviewer.

Because a resume should be custom-built, condense everything you've done into a one- or two-page document that highlights only the best and most relevant elements of your work experience. If you feel strongly about your publications, include them as a separate document which clearly highlights that it is an addendum, so it doesn't distract from your resume.

If you are struggling to stay within two pages, an easy way to save space is to cut two sections that candidates often include but add very little value to the interviewer. First, if you are using any space at the bottom of your resume to include the line, "References available upon request"—cut it. There is no situation in which an interviewer doesn't know that if they want references, they can request them.

The other section to cut is the "Objectives" section at the top of your resume. You may be using that section to include keywords that are relevant to the specific position. But embedding those keywords directly into the resume is as effective as using a block of space at the top that causes your resume to spill onto page three at the end.

Keeping the length to two pages can be difficult for a candidate with ten or more years of work experience. If you have that depth of experience, you may need to prioritize how much detail to include and where to embed it. Try to provide more information about your most recent role and reduce the details for the older roles.* Ultimately, you still may find it difficult to

---

* If your older jobs had relevant skills or experiences not captured in your most recent roles, then don't edit them out and include the most relevant details or keywords in older roles.

create a two-page resume. In those cases, a three-page resume is acceptable and not worth the work or worry about length.

Show career progression
The other quick hit that interviewers scan for is your career progression. If you've been promoted, say it in the resume. If a change from one organization to another led to a higher role in another organization, call this out with a line directly under the new role that reads:

- "Transitioned to this organization as an opportunity to progress into a role with more responsibility"

Depending on the length of your career this may not be possible. You may be early in your career with little opportunity to advance and your job titles won't reflect progression. But your descriptors in each bullet can serve a similar purpose. In that case, start some of your bullets with phrases such as:

- "Was selected to . . ."
- "Recognized for . . ."
- "Given the opportunity to . . ."

All those words indicate a version of progression. You may not have been promoted, but your supervisors saw you as someone worthy of doing more.

A well-structured, tailored resume will give you a significant advantage over candidates who don't recognize the power of the resume. It improves your odds of being advanced to an interview as well influences the questions you'll be asked. A resume structured in this way also shifts power toward you because the resume will be repeatedly reviewed at each stage of the interview process. Dedicating time on it at the front end will pay dividends as it continues to help you advance through the various stages in front of you.

This may sound like a considerable investment, but you are looking for a job that will provide income for the foreseeable future. The investment of tailoring your resume is a critical step toward that pay-off.

GIVE THE ANSWER *YOU* WANT TO GIVE

When you and the interviewer take a seat at the interview table, you both immediately enter into an agreement. No one will say it out loud, but it is an agreement that undermines the purpose of the interview. The agreement is that you are going to have answers to *every* question the interviewer asks, and the interviewer is going to play along as though you have miraculously done *every single thing* the interviewer asks about.

Every candidate wants to give honest answers. It isn't until the interview questions hit that they suddenly feel the pressure to provide examples that may not be completely true. At worst, this implicit agreement encourages candidates to lie or embellish their work experience. At best, it encourages them to morph examples of less relevant work experiences to make them more relevant to the question being asked.

The implicit agreement also has another effect. It makes the interviewer feel as though they need to get as many questions answered as possible. Whether these are great answers, average answers, answers directly related to the question, or indirectly related. Returning to their team empty-handed or with only half the questions answered isn't good for the candidate, but it also doesn't look good for the interviewer. The interviewer's job is to gather answers.

As the candidate, this implicit agreement is an opportunity to rethink the interview. It means you have something the interviewer wants. Having something someone wants, gives you power and control that you may not realize.

In the previous section we discussed how to use the resume to prime the interviewer to ask questions you will be prepared to answer. That is only a piece of the equation because the interviewer will also ask questions you weren't prepared for. But you have something the interviewer doesn't just want. You have answers—which they need. The following two practices allow you to use that to your advantage and find moments where you can give the answer you want to give, whether you were prepared for the question or not.

It is in these moments that the concept of rhetorical stance comes into play. This is when you adjust your footing by redefining the question to discuss something else in your experience that is of equal or higher quality.

The Redirect

A common mistake that interviewers make is they ask questions that signal what the answer should be. For example, interviewers often ask questions like:

> "Can you give an example of a time you convinced a co-worker to help with a project even though it wasn't a priority for them to do so?"

This example highlights several problems with the typical interview question. First, the question signals to the candidate what type of answer the interviewer is looking for. In this case, the interviewer likely wants an answer that shows your ability to convince others to help you even if they don't have time. They want to learn if you can influence others and how you react when you need help.

The second problem is related to the signaling. If you haven't done what the questions signals, you will feel tempted to do one of the following:

- Completely fabricate an answer.
- Dig into your memory for something similar and share that example.
- Take an answer you prepared for a different question and adjust that answer to fit the question asked.

All these options direct your mental energy away from giving a great answer and waste it on tweaking and making adjustments along the way. Lying is never a good option. Digging into the depths of your memory only to retrieve a less relevant answer will result in an average answer. Taking a previously prepared answer and morphing it into a new answer is the option most candidates choose because at least they can lean on their preparation. But research suggests that the interviewer will pick up signals that you are adjusting your answer. This will cause some doubt in their mind. It may even prompt follow-up questions to uncover what they are sensing.

Instead of going through this effort, you should use a technique I've seen strong candidates do. They choose Option 2, but they don't try to fool the interviewer. Instead, they acknowledge on the front end that they haven't done the exact thing being asked for—but have a very close example.

It may sound counterintuitive to acknowledge you don't have an answer. But I've seen it done, and it works. When an interviewer asks for something you haven't done:

> Interviewer: *Can you give an example of a time you convinced a co-worker to help with a project even though it wasn't a priority for them to do so?*

Think of an example that is close and ask if you can use that. For example, you might reply:

23

> Candidate: *I haven't had that exact experience. Can I give you an example of a time I had to convince someone to do something I thought they might not do?*

The reason this works is because the interviewer knows you may not have done the exact thing they asked about. That is the implicit agreement. By redirecting them to an answer you have, you are taking control and allowing both of you to momentarily step out of the agreement. From their perspective, you are giving them control to get a better answer out of you.

When candidates use this approach on me, I have to make a decision which gives them an advantage. In that moment I have several choices:

1. Tell them we have to skip that question.
2. Accept the example they give me.
3. Give them more information about what I am looking for so they can come up with an example closer to what I need.

Option 1 is unlikely because interviewers will rarely skip a question. Their job is to get answers. When you redirect, you are not refusing to answer. You are giving them what they want—an answer. Every instinct pushes them to get an answer because that is what defines them.

Option 2 is the choice most interviewers will take because even if the answer is not exactly aligned, it still gives them insight that might be valuable.

Some interviewers will choose Option 3 because they are driven to get an answer to the question they want. In this case, they have no choice but to provide even more signals to what the right answer is, which is better for you.

The third option often plays out like this:

Interviewer: *Can you give me an example of a time you had to convince a co-worker to help you with a project even though it wasn't a priority for them to do so?*

Candidate: *I haven't had that exact experience, but can I give you an example of a time I had to convince someone to do something I wasn't sure they would do?*

Interviewer: *Let's stick with this question. Another way to think about it is an example of a time you had to ask for help from others, but might not have gotten it?*

In this example, they've just signaled that they aren't just looking for an answer about influencing others. They want to know how you react when you need help but can't get it. If the interviewer takes the option of sticking with their question exactly as asked, they will often provide more information about what the right answer is.

This now gives you a few more signals. If you have a relevant example, then by all means share it. But you still may not have an experience that exactly matches that question either. Instead, use the additional information to better morph a different example into an answer for this more specific question.

"On-the-spot answer-morphing" is not the best way for an interviewer to get information about you. But if they push you in that direction, you don't have many choices. The implicit agreement requires you to figure out how to give an answer. That is your job. During an interview you can acknowledge you haven't had to deal with a scenario they've presented. But you won't last long in the process if you keep saying, "Nope, I haven't done that . . . Unfortunately, I haven't done that either . . . And also not that . . ."

Instead, try the redirecting technique. It isn't the same as saying "I haven't done that." It helps them connect the dots that you have the underlying skill, just through a different example.

The Counteroffer

The "counteroffer" is similar to redirecting, except you use it when the interviewer asks for a specific skill versus a broader example of something you've faced. The practice of counteroffering follows the exact same protocol as redirecting. It works as follows:

Interviewer: *Can you tell me about your experience using Salesforce?*

Candidate: *I haven't had the opportunity yet to work with Salesforce, but I'm very familiar with CRM systems. I've used Oracle's NetSuite and I've used Zendesk. I've learned that a lot of the underlying functions are similar. Do you mind if I tell you about my experience with those? I think the lessons learned will allow me to quickly get up to speed with Salesforce.*

Once again, you've broken the implicit agreement to your advantage. The interviewer again has three options: skip the question, accept the example, or give more signals about the answer.

As we've established, they rarely skip the question because after the interview, they'll have to report back something about that question. In this case, the question is already very specific, so they can't give more signals. What you've done is backed them into a position where they have to accept your alternative and let you share what you know about other CRMs.

This option may not sound like a great one, and it is possible that it isn't. The interviewer may want someone who has experience with Salesforce. But if that is the case, directly saying "I don't have experience with Salesforce" will have the same effect, maybe worse.

It is rare your previous job completely matches the job you are interviewing for. Interviewers know this and despite the implicit agreement, don't expect a perfect match. Your goal then is to demonstrate skills that are transferable and relevant to the job you are hiring for. Redirects and counteroffers show that your previous jobs have prepared you well for the new job.

Over the course of the interview, you need to answer some of the questions directly, but it is also as important to give examples that you can take what you've learned and adapt it. Those are moments to take control and pitch why they should consider you based on a similar skill set. If you are strong in other areas, chances are you will be viewed as a fast learner and will still be in solid running for the job.

A Word of Caution

If the position is a good fit for you, you shouldn't have to redirect or counteroffer more than two or three times during an interview. If you find that you don't have direct examples for the majority of questions asked, you may not have prepared enough, or you may need to reassess if this job is suited for you. Even though you are still giving answers when you redirect or counteroffer, repeating the strategy too many times will begin to reflect badly on you. If you find that happening, return to the implicit agreement and morph answers for those you don't have direct experience with. After the interview, invest some time determining if this job is right for you, or if you underprepared.

THE SIX THINGS EVERY INTERVIEWER WANTS

While the job description is critical to helping you prepare for (and shape) the questions asked, it is important to recognize it may not contain what managers and their teams truly want. In many organizations, the human resources department (HR) is separate from the team on which you will work. The job description HR creates will be primarily driven by the organization's needs for the open position. It won't always take into consideration the personality of the manager, unwritten rules, team dynamics, or other contextual factors that will affect you once hired.

Knowing those contextual factors can empower you and influence your answers. Access to that information would be a goldmine, because at some point your interviewers will be your future manager and people from their team. If you know someone who works inside the organization, talking to them is the best way to gain a sense of what it truly takes to do well in the role you want.

But that isn't always possible. Even when it is, be cautious about taking one person's experience as the guide for your approach to the interview. Fortunately, after having worked with many managers and their teams as they hire, I've seen a clear pattern of desired characteristics. Regardless of the role or organization, there are six common factors that all managers want to see in a candidate.

"I'm someone who is always getting better."
No interviewer wants a person who has peaked. If they believe you are strong, you want them to believe you are only going to get stronger. This is even more important if the interviewer isn't

sure if you are strong enough. They may like everything about you, but question if you have enough experience, knowledge, or some other gap they've identified. It is in those moments that the theme of "always getting better" needs to be part of how they define you. You must keep driving home the message of continuous self-improvement.

To achieve this, consistently use the following language in your answers:

- "Something I learned for the next time was . . ."
- "If I were to do this differently, I would . . ."
- "I'm always trying to get better, to do that, I would . . ."

Interviewers are often prepared to ask you questions about what you would do the next time. Those are natural places to insert these answers. But you must be prepared to share that type of response for anything you've accomplished. People often want to portray themselves as flawless, but no interviewer is looking for perfection. They know it doesn't exist, so don't waste your time going down that path. Instead, use the suggested language to acknowledge you are always learning.

The other way to demonstrate this characteristic is to consistently speak about increase in scale or scope. If you've had promotions in your career, then those easily speak to this type of growth. Depending on where you are in your career, you may not have had a promotion yet, or haven't had one recently. Regardless of your specific situation, there are natural ways to mention scale or scope and deliver the message about getting better.

- *Scale*: If you've worked on projects that have increased in budget, the number of people on the team, or any other resource required as an input, use those as examples.

- *Scope*: Similar to scale, make sure to share examples of when you've worked on projects that have had broader impact, longer timelines, cut across departments, or required more approval from higher up in the organization.

"I'm someone who gets up to speed quickly."

Whenever a person joins a team, everyone knows that person will have a lot to learn. The new hire may come in with top-notch skills and great fit with the role, but new organizational structures and relationships, different systems and processes, exposure to unwritten rules, and informal hierarchies will all be new to them.

Because of this, every manager wants someone who is a fast learner and can adjust quickly. Even if the organization has a great onboarding process and the manager dedicates time to new team members to help them adjust—few people *want* to spend their time on these things. Ideally, they want someone who demonstrates any of the following:

- The ability to quickly connect the dots and make the right assumptions.
- Doesn't get their ego bruised or get defensive when receiving feedback.
- The ability to make the necessary adjustments to improve their performance.

As a manager, bringing a new person on board is hard and takes time. Every signal you can send that demonstrates the bullets above will increase your odds of being viewed favorably.

"I'm someone who is self-aware."

Professors Daniel Cable and Virginia Kay, from the London Business School and the University of North Carolina, conducted research[4] on interviewing and identified a valuable practice known as "self-verification striving." Self-verification is the ability to convey to interviewers a picture of oneself that is more comprehensive and includes both positive and negative aspects. This research is relevant because they found that not only do interviewers gain a better understanding of candidates who strived for self-verification, the candidates then performed better in their new jobs because the manager was able to support them in ways that were most helpful.

The key to self-verification is being self-aware. Some of the best moments to demonstrate self-awareness are when asked to describe your strengths and weaknesses. This isn't always asked the same way, and is sometimes asked directly or indirectly:

- "What are your strongest skills? In which areas do you need to improve?"
- "What did you do well on that project? What could you have done better?"
- "Give me an example of your proudest accomplishment? Describe a major failure you've experienced?"
- "If you could repeat that initiative, what would you do differently?"

While they do want to assess your strengths and weaknesses, interviewers are also assessing another underlying query. The interviewer wants to know if you know yourself. Are you self-aware? Do you know what you can and can't do? Sometimes these questions are less about what you can do and more about assessing whether you know how you are perceived:

- "What would others say are your areas of strength? And your areas for potential development?"

- "When we do reference checks,* what will they say you did well in your role? And where will they say you struggled?"

Just as important as the interviewer knowing what they are getting by hiring you, they want to make sure you know what you are getting yourself into by joining their organization. People who are not self-aware struggle getting along with others, take longer to improve at their work, and are oblivious of the negative impact they have on those around them.

Be prepared to talk about both sides of you—strive to self-verify your areas of strength and your areas of development. That shows self-awareness. Interviewers will be fine with a few development areas, in particular if you are already calling them out as areas you are aware of and want to get better at.

"I'm someone who truly understands teamwork."
The concept of teamwork is used so much that it is almost cliché. But some clichés are the truth. Teamwork is one of those truths. Even roles that require little interaction are still far better done if the person can work well with others whenever needed. While teamwork is the overarching concept that everyone is familiar with, what it actually means can be unclear.

So, what does it really mean? Underneath the idea are several important factors.

Collaboration
What interviewers want to know is how well you work with others. That is defined by the following:

---

* There are many online resources with insight on preparing your reference checks. In short, let your references know they will be called, share the job description, and share key things you think are important for the job.

- The ability and willingness to share resources and information rather than hoard them.
- The ability to help others even if it isn't necessarily convenient for you.
- Comfort sharing credit and celebrating other people's success.

Whenever you are asked about teamwork, specifically talk about times you've taken any of the above actions.

Relationship-building

The second element of teamwork you must exhibit is that you can build strong relationships. During an interview, teamwork won't only be based on the quantity of your relationships— it will be based on the quality. People are far more likely to move quickly, effectively, and willingly, if they feel a personal connection with you. The importance of relationship depth is what your answers should show.

People often misinterpret relationship-building as a type of extroversion. It's a false assumption. Research[5] led by renowned Wharton professor Adam Grant has shown that introverts are particularly adept at building relationships because they are thoughtful about how they do it. In that thoughtfulness lies the answer to showing you understand relationships.

When talking about relationships, focus on moments you've spent getting to know people, individually, whether you needed them in the moment or not. If you do any of the following, make sure to share them as examples:

- Grabbing lunch or a coffee with people from *other* teams.
- Proactively offering to help colleagues in moments when they need assistance at work.

- Remembering important moments in the lives of co-workers, such as their birthday, their child's birthday, or even asking about the wellbeing of a family member who was ill.
- Exhibiting genuine interest in learning more about what brings personal happiness to your colleagues.

Relationship-building requires more than going to every happy hour and after-work function. That's often the norm and therefore won't make you stand out. What impresses interviewers is when you can show that you spend time with people on an individual level—getting to know them, providing help, and receiving it in return when you need it.

Managing conflict

Assessments of teamwork often also manifest in questions about conflict resolution. The type of conflict that matters most to interviewers is conflict with colleagues and conflict with customers. You must show that you can work with difficult people and still advance the goal. For co-workers, be prepared with answers for the following types of questions:

- "Have you ever had a colleague with whom you differed in opinion? How did you manage that?"
- "Do you have an example of a difficult relationship you've had to manage with a co-worker?"
- "What is the most challenging work relationship you've had? What caused it? How did it impact your work?"

You don't need three different answers for these questions. You need one answer that gets at the core of the questions—demonstrating how you work with people who are difficult. Prepare that answer and then no matter which format the question arrives in, you'll be ready.

If you are in a role that will deal with customers, partners, vendors, or other external stakeholders, the same three types of question apply, just with the external focus:

- "Have you ever had a customer/vendor/partner with whom you disagreed? How did you manage that?"
- "Do you have an example of a difficult situation you've had to manage with a customer/vendor/partner?"
- "What is the most challenging customer/vendor/partner experience you've had? What caused it? How did it end?"

Again, you don't need three different answers for these questions. Develop one answer that gets at the core of the questions and you'll be prepared.

"I'm someone who is resilient."
Managers want people who don't break easily, bounce back, and keep pushing for results regardless of difficulties they face. What they are looking for is resilience. When your resilience is being assessed, it can be best demonstrated in two ways.

Ability to recover from failures or mistakes
On a recent trip to visit with leaders at X Development (formerly Google X), a speaker shared with me that when it comes to assessing talent, they were less interested in failure avoidance and more interested in error recovery. We all know that mistakes happen. What interviewers want are people who don't let mistakes or fear of mistakes stop them. Questions in this category are often along the following lines:

35

- "Do you have an example of a time you failed? What did you learn from it?"
- "What do you consider your biggest failure? What would you do differently?"

The second part of the question is the most important part of that question because it gives you the opportunity to demonstrate your ability to recover. That second part may not always be asked by the interviewer. Even when not asked, the interviewer is still trying to get a feel for your ability to learn, your self-awareness, and whether you can bounce back from mistakes. Regardless of how the question is framed, if they ask about failure, always discuss recovery in your answer.

Ability to juggle multiple responsibilities
There are few jobs in which you only do one thing. In today's workforce, everyone from COOs to assembly line workers are being cross-trained to play multiple roles. If you have any aspirations of moving up in the workforce, don't expect to only do one thing.

The surest way to plateau is to focus only on single domain expertise. In today's competitive, fast-moving world, employers want people who can take on multiple tasks or work streams at the same time. Expect to be asked questions that fall along these lines:

- "When juggling multiple things at once, how do you decide what gets top priority?"
- "Has there been a time when you were overloaded with work? Were you able to get it done on time, and if not, how did you decide what to de-prioritize?"
- "Tell me about two to three work streams you are responsible for in your current job?"

You'll notice many of these questions are about your ability to prioritize and manage your time. You'll often hear questions with themes of time management, prioritization, tight deadlines, and/or too much work.

These questions are all versions of the same trait that managers want to see. They all want to know if you can effectively do more than one thing at once. Prepare several examples about juggling multiple projects, work streams, or responsibilities and you'll be prepared for a wide range of questions regardless of how they are worded.

"I'm someone who works hard."

There is no shortage of maxims about "working smart" as well as advice about "work-life balance." But the word "work" is integral to those maxims. Put simply, employers still want people who work hard. If you are working smart, that does not imply that an employer doesn't want you to work hard and use those smarts to get more done than the competitor. If you want work-life balance, that is important. But no employer wants the work portion of that balance to somehow equate to less performance.

During the early stages of the interview process, the signal you want to send is that you work hard. Those questions often come in the form of:

- "Do you have an example of a time you took on a project even though it wasn't your priority?"
- "Do you have an example of a time when you achieved a great deal in a short amount of time?"
- "What drives you to do great work?"

You will want to make sure you know your personal boundaries and needs for balance. But those types of conversations either come after you've received an offer or in later stages of the interview process when they are more invested in hiring you. Knowing the culture of the organization can help you determine how open to be about your boundaries, whether you should include it in an answer, and when.

While this suggested strategy of waiting to share your perspective on work-life balance is generally the better approach, your specific circumstances could require you to be open about the balance you need early on. If you need balance that restricts how much you can work, and the role being interviewed for doesn't help reach that goal—it's better to learn that on the front end and not advance, than land the job and be miserable.

You want to avoid your work ethic being called into question, but your physical and mental health is more important than any strategy I can recommend. Always err on the side that is most applicable to your specific context.

HOW MANY ANSWERS SHOULD YOU PREPARE?

One of the complexities of being a candidate is not knowing how many different answers and stories to have mentally stockpiled. If you search around for insight on this, it's hard to come by. However, as an experienced interviewer, I can tell you that it's best to prepare twelve to sixteen answers. That probably sounds very high. It's intimidating to think that you need to create that many. But before brushing it off, let's think about what you likely have already prepared:

- Three to five skills you want to demonstrate
- Three to five traits you want to demonstrate
- One story that answers "Tell me about yourself"

From these alone you are already at seven to eleven answers. The only additional answers to prepare are ones you can pull directly from your resume. Since your resume is custom-built, every bullet aligns with the role you are interviewing for and was intentionally included from your experiences. The resume alone carries at least another five stories that may not have been captured in the list above. Now you can see how quickly you've landed at twelve to sixteen answers.

This isn't as bad as it seems. These aren't answers you've made up from scratch. They are work you've done and accomplishments you've achieved that you can speak to. Your next step is to jot them down and apply either a logical or storytelling framework to each of them. Which is what we'll discuss in the next two sections.

INTERVIEWERS LOVE LOGIC

The next two sections focus on specific structures—logic and story—which give you the ability to consistently provide strong responses during an interview. Each structure represents a different way to provide an answer. Each will have techniques associated with it from which you can choose, depending on your preferences.

Providing a structure to your answers is based on a concept called "processing fluency." In short, the more structured your answer is, the clearer it is and the better the listener can process what they are hearing. According to Stanford Communication professor Matt Abrahams, listeners process structured information 40 percent more effectively than unstructured information.[6] Structure helps people remember what they heard.

This connection between structure and processing fluency goes even deeper than the interviewer's ability to understand and remember what you say. Researchers at the University of Michigan[7] found how well a person processes what you are saying also affects how they *feel* about you. As humans, we are constantly judging one another, often without knowing it and without knowing the source of that judgment. The research, however, discovered a direct relationship between how well someone understands you and their eventual judgment of you. In the context of interviewing, it is important to know that the more easily the interviewer processes what you are saying:

- The more familiar you will feel to them and their connection to you will be stronger.
- The less risk they will associate with you. When processing is difficult, the perception of risk goes up.
- The more they will trust the answer given. Similar to risk, the harder it is to understand an answer, the more likely it is that the interviewer will question the truth of the answer.

The effect of processing fluency has been replicated in multiple studies,[8] which makes it even more important to use specific structures that drive the interview toward the outcome you want. We'll begin by focusing first on logic.

Logic as Structure

The art of persuasion is central to this book, but it didn't begin in 1963 with Professor Wayne C. Booth. Its history goes back thousands of years, with the most cited lessons coming from philosophers in ancient Greece. Plato was one of those philosophers, but he didn't view persuasion very positively. He viewed it primarily in the context of politics and felt it was used to unfairly influence the "ignorant masses."

Aristotle, Plato's student and eventually his colleague, saw things differently. He saw persuasion as a mechanism for proving any important point. Aristotle believed it was applicable beyond just the realms of politics and law, where motives were suspect, and felt it could be applied across many fields: art, architecture, cartography, history, and even religion. He believed in order to effectively persuade anyone, you had to know how to use a specific set of tools—ethos, pathos, and logos.

While a deep dive into a lesson on Greek philosophy isn't necessary, a quick reminder of the terms is helpful. Ethos is when you use credibility to make your point. The more credible you make yourself to the listener, the more likely they are to believe you. Pathos is the use of emotion to make a point. Logos, on the other hand, is when the speaker uses logic or reason to prove a point. The power of ethos, pathos, and logos has been used for centuries and can absolutely be applied to the interview setting as you help the interviewer understand why you are the best person for the job.

Throughout this book, you will find approaches built on these time-tested elements. In this section, you'll learn how to structure answers so the logical conclusion is that you have the desired skills. By the time the interview is over, *not* hiring you should seem *illogical* and doing so would go against the interviewer's best reasoning.

COMPARISON

Interviewers don't have much information on which to base decisions when they meet you. If it is the first interview, they've been influenced by your resume and any additional research they've done on you. Beyond the first interview, the interviewer is primarily reliant on your words. The way you structure your words can influence the logical side of the interviewer's decision-making processes. These structures won't require you to speak in a way that seems abnormal because they are based on the way the human brain normally functions.

A strong answer structure you can use is based on a theory in psychology called "Social Comparison Theory." This concept suggests that people, across a wide range of areas, have a hard time assessing themselves. In those moments, when we are trying to determine how we are performing, we compare ourselves to others. This gives us a marker against which to measure whether we are doing well or not.

The same use of comparison as a measurement applies when we judge other people. As I've trained interviewers over the years, one of the practices we teach is that interviewers should never compare candidates against each other. To make better decisions, they should only compare candidates to the job criteria and desired skills. The reason we do this training is because our brains are wired to compare people to each other. It is the simpler thing to do.

That natural default in decision-making is what you will tap into with the following technique.

"Better Than"

The practice is straightforward. When giving an answer, find moments when you can reference how you are better than someone else at whatever the topic is.

> Interviewer: *Do you have an example of a time when you led a project with a limited budget?*

> Candidate: *Last year we had to find savings of 20 percent across three departments. I led this with a colleague, and we realized that I was stronger at the analytical side of the work. We were both good at implementation and relationship-building, but my experience with budget-building was deeper than my colleague's, so we divided the work in that way. We had about two months to accomplish . . .*

When you prepare answers for potential questions, have a few examples where you can highlight the moments when you were stronger than someone else. The structure does not require you to say someone else dropped the ball or was a poor performer. You are not throwing anyone under the bus nor bragging. The best way to do this is to use examples where:

- A division of labor was necessary, and you took work that catered to your strength.
- The stakes were high, and the best person was needed.

An example of the second option above would be:

> Interviewer: *Do you have an example of a time when you led a project with a limited budget?*

Candidate: *Last year we had to find savings of nearly 20 percent across three departments. I led this with a colleague, and there were incredibly high stakes. We had a tight timeline of about six weeks. Because of that, we identified that I should take on the analysis portion because we both were strong on implementation and relationship-building, but my experience with number crunching was a clear strength compared to his. We started the project by* . . .

In both examples, the candidate organically positioned themselves as stronger in analysis. They gave the interviewer enough context to justify that statement. The logical side of the interviewer's brain—relying on comparison—is designed to accept that this candidate is stronger at analysis. This alone won't be enough to make the case that your analytical ability is strong, but you've planted an important seed about your skills. Later, when the interviewers are making a decision based on the information they've gathered on their candidates, those seeds will be part of a decision in your favor.

SOCIAL PROOF

Interviews are filled with paradoxes and complexities. One of them is that an interview requires you to speak highly of yourself. But if you speak too highly of yourself, you sound like you are bragging. In general, arrogance isn't viewed positively and can hurt your chances of advancing.

As a candidate, this requires you to balance sharing everything that is great about you without turning people off. Part of this balance is accomplished by including areas of development and acknowledging mistakes you've made. But at multiple points, you will have to speak highly of yourself. Those moments must feel credible and as unbiased as possible.

Using comparison is one approach. A similar practice is built on a principal in psychology known as "social proof." This theory, popularized by psychologist and marketing professor Robert Cialdini, has shown that when people are uncertain of what to believe, they look to the actions and preferences of others. They then mirror those actions because they accept them as proof of what is true and accurate.

You can leverage "social proof" in answers by sharing your strengths from the perspective of how others view you. Two answer structures can be used to this end:

"I have a reputation for . . ."
During an interview, you will likely be asked to share your strengths and weaknesses. Those aren't the times to be shy. Have an answer prepared that highlights what you are really good at and your areas of development. As long as you provide both sides, you don't need to worry about arrogance.

But you need to continue reinforcing your strengths throughout the interview without sounding arrogant. One mechanism is to insert the phrase, "I have a reputation for" into answers. This can help drive home the message about your strengths. For example:

Interviewer: *Do you have an example of how you handled a difficult situation with a client/customer?*

Candidate: *A client recently wanted us to deliver a project with a deadline that our organization thought could impact the quality of the work. The client had a long relationship with us and we couldn't afford to lose her. I've managed to build a reputation as a strong project manager in our organization. Those moments when we are under the gun, are the moments when people ask me to help figure out what is possible. So, I was asked to join this project . . .*

This example makes it clear the candidate's strength is project management. The candidate is sharing this, but in a way that is validated by their colleagues. They are sharing it as though it is already a known fact among many. The language is subtle, but it lends credibility to the candidate and highlights their strength via a neutral third party.

"One of the things I'm known for . . ."
For some people, the phrase "I have a reputation for" feels a little too heavy-handed. You have to know yourself and what language fits you best. If that phrase feels too close to arrogance, then instead use simpler language and say, "One of the things I'm known for . . ."

Here is the exact same scenario, but with different wording:

Interviewer: *Do you have an example of how you handled a difficult situation with a client/customer?*

Candidate: *A client recently wanted us to deliver a project with a deadline that our organization thought could impact the quality of the work. The client had a long relationship with us and we couldn't afford to lose her. One of the things I'm known for in our organization is project management. Those moments when we are under the gun, are the moments when people ask me to help figure out what is possible. So, I was asked to join this project . . .*

The goal of these tactics is to find a natural way to continue showing your strengths throughout the interview. Logic helps you do this successfully. If you simply keep describing your strengths in first-person, the logical side of the interviewer's brain will conclude, "This candidate is biased to only say good things about themselves. Logically, I should question whether they are accurately portraying themselves."

But if you present your strengths through the eyes of others, the internal logic is different. Even though you are reporting what others think of you, this structure strengthens your odds of being viewed as credible. The logic is now, "Other people think highly of this candidate's skills. It seems logical I should as well."

By introducing third parties in your answers, you are providing someone after whom the interviewer can model their own beliefs about you and your skills.

APPEAL TO AUTHORITY

When our brains seek information on which to base a decision, we often turn to some authority figure to help make the determination. This doesn't only apply to whether something is true but also to whether something is of high quality or not. If someone with authority determines something is of value, then we tend to also believe that it is of value.

In the scholarly world this is called "*argumentum ad verecundiam*" and there is disagreement about whether using this approach is a valid way to win an argument. This is an academic debate only scholars would engage in because in real-life situations, it doesn't matter. An appeal to authority is based on the concept of social proof and what matters is that our brains are wired to accept them.

Interviewers like examples with tangible results you can speak to. They prefer these examples because they need something concrete to help them judge if you've done good work. The reality for you as a candidate is that you won't always have tangible results, data, or the type of answers that provide that security. In those moments, the alternative is to find examples of projects for which you received approval or praise from a superior. For example:

Interviewer: *Can you give me an example of a time you successfully completed a project ahead of schedule?*

When you share your answer to a question like this, the interviewer feels like they must take your word that you completed it ahead of schedule. Depending on how well you delivered the answer, they may believe you or they may have doubts.

To reduce those doubts, use examples in which a superior acknowledged the great work you did. A strong answer to the question above would be structured so it gives an example of when you completed a project ahead of schedule and it would end with the following sentence:

> Candidate: . . . *One of the other benefits of finishing ahead of the timeline, was the recognition we received from our supervisor. She knew we were under a time crunch and she was impressed by what we accomplished in such a short amount of time.*

These simple few lines cause the interviewer to give your answer more credibility than before. They don't know your supervisor—but they represent an authority figure who has determined your work is good work.

The logic flow is that if your boss believed the work was impressive, then it likely was impressive. By adding the line, you increase the odds the interviewer will recall it as a strong example of your ability to do what is required in the role.

SELF-IDENTITY

A common characteristic that defines us all is our desire to have our individual identity affirmed, known, or valued. Generally, people want to be seen and accepted for who they are. Identity is something sacred and important. How a person chooses to identify tells us a lot about that person. In most cases, we give people the benefit of the doubt when they self-identify in a certain way. This element of human behavior is the foundation for another strategy that can be used to strengthen an answer. Here is an example:

> Interviewer: *Can you share a time when you built a relationship in a short amount of time?*

> Candidate: *In my previous role, I was working on a project in which we partnered with the local chamber of commerce. We had to build relationships quickly. I'm the type of person who values establishing trust with people I'm working with, and that accelerates relationships. On this project . . .*

In that answer, did you catch the self-identity strategy? It's the part of the answer where the candidate says, "I'm the type of person who . . ." This seems subtle, but the most effective forms of influence are subtle. By using this phrase, you have made the ability to establish trust as part of your identity. The instinct in all of us, including interviewers, is to accept self-identification as truth. This gives your answer more power and shapes their view of you.

This strategy can also be used to make it clear who you are *not*. The same question could unfold as follows.

> Interviewer: *Can you share a time when you built a relationship in a short amount of time?*

> Candidate: *In my previous role, I was working on a project in which we partnered with the local chamber of commerce. We had to build relationships quickly. I am not the type of person who wastes time in any way. Trust is a great way to build a relationship, so I immediately reached out to talk to . . .*

In this case, the candidate identified themselves as someone who does not waste time.* The interviewer will remember that aspect of the candidate's identity and will continue to view them through that lens unless given a reason not to.

Providing a few answers where you either identify yourself as someone who does X or as someone who would never do Y, is a natural and effective way to show the interviewer who you are or what you stand for. It builds a perception of you that will stay with them well after the interview and into the moments when they make a hiring decision. That perception you've created is exactly what you want the interviewers to be thinking about as they deliberate.

A Word of Caution

The practices we've shared so far—social proof, appeal to authority, and self-identity—can all be over-used and cause the opposite of what you want. Your desired outcome is to share

---

* Trust-building is also being shared as part of the candidate's identity in this example.

your strengths without seeming arrogant. But if you use *all* these tactics, you will definitely come across as arrogant.

Imagine if, during the course of a single interview, you told the interviewer that you are better than a colleague, have an outstanding reputation, have a boss who admires you, and that you self-identify as highly skilled. Any one of these alone is subtle. If you do them all at once in an interview, then you are clearly bragging.

To successfully use these techniques, first determine which ones feel most natural to you. Then during any one interview, only use two of them. Across multiple interviews, you can keep using the strategies, but no more than twice within any given interview. This allows you to develop a theme around your strengths without reaching the point of arrogance.

These approaches are meant to be subtle nudges, pushing the interviewer toward viewing your answers as strong and credible, and keeping their assessment of you positive. When you are influencing, it is nudges, not heavy-handedness, that will shift opinions in your favor.

TALKING POINTS AND LISTS

The Law School Admission Test (LSAT) is the half-day exam that must be passed in order to be admitted into law school. The LSAT consists of six sections, and three of them test the candidate's ability to think logically. A lawyer's success is built around persuading others to reach a specific opinion, and an understanding of logic allows them to structure compelling and coherent arguments. Those arguments can be made by deliberate word choice, such as the techniques mentioned so far in this chapter. They can further be enhanced by boiling the message into a set of talking points or using a list structure to drive home a point. Successful courtroom lawyers know the value of a logical delivery of a message, which makes their profession perfect to draw the following lessons from.

Use Talking Points, Not a Script

Strong lawyers know their job is not to cover everything. In their preparation they determine what they need to cover, and just as importantly, what facts, elements, and information to discard. As a candidate, the way to accomplish this is to prepare all the answers and examples you plan to give, including the details. But don't plan to deliver the detailed version of your notes. Instead, create an outline only with the high-level points you want to make.

As you prepare answers, think of yourself as a sculptor. Start with more information than necessary and whittle down to the essence of your answer. What you want are phrases that capture that essence. Those talking points keep you from deviating away from the core of your answer.

You want to memorize talking points, not entire answers. Memorizing an entire answer is one of the hardest, most time-consuming, and ineffective activities you can do. If you rehearse every single line of your answers, you will feel and sound stilted. To make things worse, memorizing an answer will only heighten your anxiety if, during the interview, you don't recall something. It is in those moments where you begin to improvise and ramble.

Lawyers are great at identifying their key points and driving them home consistently. That is what you are after as well. An outline with key phrases will serve as easy-to-follow markers that remind you of details that you can fill in. This format makes the amount you need to recall much less and allows you to shuffle points around more easily to fit whatever question is asked of you.

Talk in Lists

When you study how lawyers speak and how they use talking points to drive home a point, you will find an interesting theme. Many of them speak in lists. In other words, they make it very easy to follow their argument by speaking almost as though they are listing bullet points. They will make their first point and say, "The first thing you'll notice . . ." This will then be followed by, "Second, it's important to keep in mind . . .," followed by "Lastly, it became clear . . ."

Taking your talking points and using them as a list gives you several advantages. First, the list structure minimizes deviations. Once you've identified the issue you want to address, stay on that issue. Lists allow you to hammer away, blow after blow. Second, our brains are trained to follow sequences,[9] so answering in a list format makes it easier to remember and deliver your main points. Third, the same is true on the receiving end. The interviewer will also more easily comprehend your answer and they are more likely to recall your answer later as concise and well-organized.

An overlooked aspect of being a good candidate is helping the interviewer do their job. If you make it easier for the interviewer to take notes, understand your thinking, or stay engaged, you automatically move up a notch in their mind. In my experience as an interviewer, it is much easier to follow and take notes when a candidate talks in lists. Most interviewers don't realize this technique makes them favor candidates who use it, but the science behind processing fluency has proven it to be true.

INTERVIEWERS LOVE STORIES

In the previous chapter, we shared techniques lawyers use to effectively make an argument. Anyone who has practiced law would quickly point out that logic alone won't win a case. The best lawyers know they must also rely on their ability to construct a good story, particularly if they can appeal to emotion. This is what scholars call "pathos."

According to anthropologists, storytelling is an ancient practice and part of the way our brains operate. For centuries, storytelling has been used to share information, set norms, explain phenomena, entertain, attract, and teach. Children tell stories from the moment they begin to string words together. They tell stories about what they saw or things they don't understand. They often tell stories to themselves as they play.

Stories are a definitive marker of the human experience because of their ability to reveal patterns and create structure. They make sense of the world around us. They help our minds follow a path of breadcrumbs, snapping up each one until we arrive where the storyteller wants us to arrive.

In 1944, psychologists Fritz Heider and Marianne Simmel did a simple experiment[10] to better understand how our minds work. In the experiment, they showed a simple animated film in which two triangles, a circle, and a rectangle move around each other, and in and out of the rectangle. They showed this video to thirty-four subjects and ask them to describe what they saw.

Only one of the subjects described the video for what it was, just shapes moving around on a screen. Every other participant in the experiment humanized the shapes and turned what was happening in the video into a story. This reaction is more than simply associating films with stories. This experiment has been repeated many times in a wide range of formats and environments. Every time, people automatically create a story to explain what is going on.

As a candidate, understanding that the human mind always creates stories is important, because it means one of two things. Either you structure your answers with the narrative you want—or the interviewer will. It is in your best interest to keep control of the narrative, because allowing the interviewer to create a story about you may not result in the ending you want.

Research out of Harvard[11] has shown that stories build familiarity and trust and they make the listener more willing to learn. Kendall Haven is an internationally renowned expert on the science of story structure. According to Haven:

> "Your goal in every communication is to influence your target audience (change their current attitudes, belief, knowledge, and behavior). Information alone rarely changes any of these. Research confirms that well-designed stories are the most effective vehicle for exerting influence."

Part of your success rests on your ability to tell your story. This doesn't mean you must become a master storyteller. Doing great in an interview will not require you to become the next Steven Spielberg, Terry McMillan, or Aesop. Rather, what you need to learn is a set of simple rules to follow when providing an answer.

THE HERO'S JOURNEY

Stories are such an engrained part of our cognitive machinery that we no longer even recognize the power they hold. To put that power in perspective, it's worth recognizing that stories are the reason censorship exists. The ability for stories to influence is the reason certain books have been banned or even burned. The same can be said about a range of other mediums for telling stories, all of which are controlled to ensure certain content doesn't influence certain people. For example, the influential power of stories is why the rating system for movies exists (Rated G, PG, R, etc.).

While books and radio at one time held the most sway over what people believe, today that power lives squarely in Hollywood. In our modern society, our love for stories is evident in the monumental success of Netflix. Their endless programming on nearly every topic has put countless stories at our fingertips, and as a result they have become one of the most successful media companies ever.

The storytellers in Hollywood have perfected the art of engaging the listener and persuading them to believe what they want them to believe. So, it is there we will learn our first lesson about how to deliver an answer that will sway your listener in the direction you want.

The power of most stories rests on a structure called "the Hero's Journey." This structure, also called "the monomyth," has its roots in anthropology, where cultural anthropologist Sir Edward Burnett Tylor began to document patterns in the journey of heroes. This was later picked up by psychologists and mythologists, and eventually made its way into a formal structure for effectively telling stories.

The Hero's Journey structure is complex and includes twelve different stages. Each stage represents a shift in the narrative or a milestone the main character reaches. During an interview, you do *not* need to work through twelve stages of an answer. Fortunately, the stages are broken into three main "acts." That three-act structure is most relevant for you as the candidate. For the purpose of interviewing, they are:

- *The setup*: The part of the answer where you provide some context. Perhaps this is background information, some facts about the organization, a sense of the resources you had on hand, etc.
- *The struggle*: This is the part of the answer where you articulate the problem or issue you faced. In the Hero's Journey, this is what the hero must eventually overcome, and where you explain how you overcame the hurdle you faced.
- *The closing*: This is the end of the story and highlights what results came out of this journey. This may be the outcomes, your own growth, or benefits to the team or organization. This portion is the finale and you want the utmost clarity on what you accomplished.

This structure is what you need to remember when answering any behavioral interview question. Behavioral questions are those in which you are asked for an example of something you've done. They always begin with some version of:

- "Give me an example of . . ."
- "Can you think of a time when you . . ."
- "Have you had an experience where you . . ."
- "Have you ever . . ."
- "What have you done when faced with . . ."

All the frameworks in this section are designed to answer these types of questions. Below you will find three different versions of the Hero's Journey. The idea is not to memorize each one. Instead, review them and find the style that best suits your personality and communication style. Once you've identified it, practice giving most of your answers with that structure.

STAR METHOD

The STAR method is the most well-known framework for answering a behavioral question. "STAR" is an acronym for the four pieces you should include in a strong answer.

1. *Situation*: Explain the situation you were in. Quickly provide a few of the important details. Maybe the budget, the people you worked with, who assigned the project, and/or why it was important.
2. *Task*: Describe the role you played in this situation. Explain what it was you were tasked to do.
3. *Action*: Describe the challenge and what you did to address it. Describe the hurdles and how you dealt with them. Even if you stumbled, that's okay, that's part of the story.
4. *Results*: Finally, share what came out of this struggle. Share what you accomplished and/or learned.

You'll notice that STAR is a four-act structure. But it is still the Hero's Journey because the STAR structure takes the first act—the setup—and breaks it into Situation and Task. Those two pieces then lead into Action, and then Results.

The next frameworks follow the same story arc but follow the more traditional three-part structure.

PROBLEM. SOLUTION. BENEFIT

W e each tell stories differently, so your answers can be told with lines slightly blurred. That is the case with "Problem. Solution. Benefit." This structure shifts the line between setup and struggle as well as between solution and benefit. I share this because it might fit your personality better or might resonate more with you as a storyteller. But the underlying pattern remains, which is important because it is familiar to listeners.

1. *Problem*: Share the problem you faced, and in doing so, you'll have to share enough context for them to understand the problem.
2. *Solution*: Explain the solution you provided to address the issue you faced. It is also always helpful to explain why you landed on this solution.
3. *Benefits*: Finally, close the story with the outcomes and how they benefited you, the team, or the organization. Similar to STAR, those outcomes can be accomplishments and/or learnings.

The word "problem" sometimes confuses candidates when they think about this structure. But "problem" simply means the thing the interviewer wants to know how you handled. It may not have been an actual problem, but in the Hero's Journey there is always something you had to do that wasn't easy or immediately solvable.

WHAT. SO WHAT. NOW WHAT.

The structure of "What. So What. Now What." is very similar to the other two, but for some people this approach suits them better. Based on how you communicate, this style may flow more easily and therefore lend itself to how you tell stories.

1. *What*: This is the context, the background, who was involved, etc.
2. *So What*: This is a twist on the struggle piece of the Hero's Journey. The problem or issue exists in this part and you are helping the interviewer understand why it matters or why it was particularly difficult or important. This heightens their understanding of what you faced and draws them into the story.
3. *Now What*: Finally, you get to close the story with what happened, but this version has a bit of a future orientation to it. It again focuses not just on the solution, but why this solution matters.

This structure taps more into our desire to want to know "why" something happened and "why" the results matter. The Hero's Journey is at the core of all these techniques. You don't have to pick one. If you are comfortable telling stories, use more than one of these structures as you see fit. But if you aren't a natural storyteller, then pick one and stick with it. When you choose the one that best fits your style, your story will flow better. Don't worry about it feeling repetitive. Each answer you give will have different context, different struggles and different closing, so it feels more natural than you'd assume.

The Hero's Journey is at the core of almost every story, every movie, every book, every podcast. All of them built on this very same structure. We innately think in the form of storytelling, and the best stories have some type of tension.

Your job is to use one of the structures, build some tension, and then release it. It will *feel* like what people want to hear. It will be a good story they know how to follow. A story they will remember. And at the end—you will be the hero. Flawed and imperfect, but nevertheless, the one who emerged stronger and better. That is the person they will want on their team.

HOW TO ANSWER "TELL ME ABOUT YOURSELF"

Many interviews will begin with a simple question, "So, tell me a little about yourself." It seems like a natural way to ease into a conversation. After all, you know your own story well, so the stakes shouldn't feel too high.

Yet, somehow, that isn't how it feels. When presented with that question, you'll likely wonder what the interviewer is really looking for. You'll second guess how much of yourself to reveal. Where you grew up? Your hobbies? Whether you have kids? You won't be sure where to even begin your story. At birth? At the start of college? Or you'll wonder if this isn't meant to be a literal question. Maybe you need to somehow show who you are as a human being.

Suddenly the options seem endless and seven minutes later you've rambled about everything from your grandmother's hardware store to your volunteer work at the zoo.

The reality is that interviewers want to know a little bit of all of the above and then some. They want to hear some of your life story. They want insight on what you stand for. They also want to see how well you communicate. What they are really asking is, "Who are you?" And they want that information in a relatively short answer. It isn't meant to be a hardball question but a long-winded answer without a purpose can start you off at a deficit.

Fortunately, it isn't as difficult to answer as it sounds. But like any other question, if you don't prepare—you will stumble. A strong answer to "Tell me about yourself," is designed to make you memorable and has the following four building blocks:

- Where you grew up
- A detail or two about where you grew up, e.g.:
    o Something about your family
    o Your high school
    o Characteristics of your neighborhood
- If you went to college, naming where and why.
    o If you didn't go to college, naming your first job and why you took it
- A more recent piece of information to finish the answer, e.g.:
    o Where you currently work or live
    o If applicable, your current status as a parent our spouse

Unless you are a gifted storyteller, this isn't the time for the Quentin Tarantino version of your life with a non-linear story, jumping back and forth between present and past. Tell your story in chronological order. That will be easier for you to remember and easier for the interviewer to follow.

The other common mistake to avoid is trying to tie your professional skills into your personal story. You will have the entire interview to talk about your expertise. This answer is about making a brief memorable connection that provides an initial glimpse of you beyond your resume. To accomplish that, stick to the structure above and use it to share something unique and share some of your values.

Something Unique
Think about the four building blocks you would share for you answer and determine one or two that have a unique story behind them. This does not mean you need to have an unbelievably exceptional story to tell. You just need to find an element of your story that sets you apart. Perhaps you grew up in

a town with unique name, or on a street with a unique name. Maybe your high school has a distinctive mascot, reputation, or location. Or maybe your spouse, parent, or other relative has a relatively rare profession.

This approach utilizes a cognitive bias called the Von Restorff Effect. Also known as the isolation effect, it is leveraged by everyone from advertisers to website designers and is the reason we highlight text when we want to remember something we are reading. Discovered in 1933 by German psychiatrist Hedwig von Restorff, this concept identified a human tendency that shouldn't be surprising—we are more likely to remember something when it stands out from its peers.

Advertisers often use a different tone, visual or color to make a selection standout that they want the consumer to choose. Website designers will place a default pricing plan in the center of other options and make it slightly more prominent. The Von Restorff Effect causes the listener's brain to pay more attention and the unique element is not only noticed in the present but remembered afterward as well.

When telling your story, you need to do the same. Find something that turns the four building blocks from the generic template they could easily become, into a story only you could tell. Sharing one or two distinctive elements makes you stand out from your peers. It will have the desired effect of making you less of a cut-out, more human, and easier to remember.

Your Values

The other opportunity this question presents is a moment to highlight some of your values. Values are generally interpreted to be your guiding principles, fundamental beliefs, or standards of behavior. That definition may feel too philosophical to be useful in this context. A better way to grasp what you want to share is to simply think of your values as the things that you believe are important in life.

Sharing your values is important for the same reason sharing something unique is important, it makes you stand out. During an interview, most candidates discuss their skills, strengths, areas of development, their interest in the role, etc. Very few discuss their values. By proactively using the question "Tell me about yourself," to share your values you are once again humanizing yourself and connecting on a deeper level. You are becoming memorable.

Don't get bogged down in overthinking your values. You'll use broad strokes to paint this part of the picture. Keep it simple and just think about what is important to you. Family. Faith. Discipline. Work Ethic. Once you have that list, try to determine where those values originated from. It is likely you'll find they come from a place close to one of the four building blocks. They were probably shaped by where you grew up, family members, or experiences you've had in school or work. Reflecting on those values allows you to organically connect them to the story you will tell.

Here is an example of what the answer looks like when it's all pulled together.

Interviewer: *So, tell me about yourself.*

Candidate: *I grew up in the same house that my father grew up in. Not only that, but my grandparents still lived there with all of us. It was an interesting childhood being so close to my grandparents, I even shared a bedroom with my grandfather during a brief period when my grandmother was angry with him and kicked him out of their room. We lived in Camden, New Jersey. Philadelphia was close and when it was time for college, I ended up at*

UPenn. They have a strong business school and I knew that was the direction I was headed. Entrepreneurship was interesting to me at the time, but I ended up working in a more traditional organization. My first job was with Bank of America. I actually worked there as a teller in college to make ends meet and after grad school ended up working in corporate. I recently moved here to the Bay Area, which coincidentally is where my grandparents met. They are the ones I credit for instilling in me my belief in hard work and focus, as well as commitment to taking care of family. Ending up back here in the Bay Area has really been a great way for me to reconnect with my memories of them as well as take this next step in my career.

This example uses the four building blocks and weaves in something unique and memorable (growing up with grandparents) as well as highlights some of the candidate's values.

The four bullets that serve as the structure for your answer are not complicated. As it stands, anyone can tell this type of story. But when you take that structure and use it to convey something different along with several values, you'll have an answer the interviewer will feel a stronger connection to and will remember.

That is the effect you want to have. Later, when the interviewers are discussing your interview, whether you were memorable will impact whether you advance. I have been in many of those discussions that happen post-interview. When a candidate is mentioned because of something that made them stand out, it puts them back into the conversation, and they are suddenly being discussed when others are not. Your answer to "Tell me about yourself," is an important opportunity to plant yourself firmly in the interviewer's memory, which will nudge you a step closer to the job offer you are pursuing.

USE LOGIC, STORY, OR BOTH?

The previous two sections have been focused on using logic and storytelling to convey your perspective and to persuade the interviewer you're a good fit for the job. If you aren't sure which approach to use, then return to the advice from the opening chapter on how to use this book—use context and time to help you decide.

In this case, "context" means your personal preferences. For some people, the techniques captured in the logic section will feel more natural, for others the storytelling approach is better suited. Let that be your guide.

If you still aren't sure, then time should drive your strategy. If you have time to practice, cognitive science suggests you should consider using both logic and storytelling as techniques. Your brain consists of two parts—the right hemisphere and the left hemisphere—and we've been taught they are responsible for different functions. The right is primarily responsible for creativity, imagination, and intuition. The left controls tasks related to analytical thought, reasoning, and language. Recent research indicates this isn't entirely true. There is a third part of the brain that is less commonly discussed called the "*corpus callosum.*" It sits between the two hemispheres and integrates the various cognitive functions between both sides.

The brain is much more integrated than we would think. No one thinks only analytically or creatively. Both sides of the brain impact decision-making. As a candidate, the answers you provide should take advantage of how interviewers think. When possible, your responses should appeal to both reasoning and imagination. Your best answers will be those that appeal to their logic and they should also tell a story.

Unfortunately, time isn't always on our side. If you don't have much time to practice, then pick one of the Hero's Journey structures from the story section and the "Talk in Lists" technique as suggested in the logic section. Those two techniques are the simplest to learn in a short amount of time and you can quickly apply them to your next interview.

It's fine if you can't draw both logic and story into your preparation, don't let that bother you. What is most important is that you understand the power of structure when you prepare an answer. Use logic. Use story. Or use both. As long as you leverage structure, you'll be ahead of the candidates who don't understand either.

CLARITY

Whether you choose logic, stories, or a mix of both, the outcome of your interview will be heavily influenced by your clarity of communication. This brings us back to the concept of processing fluency. As you may recall, processing fluency means the clearer your answer—the better the listener can understand what you are saying. This seems obvious, but science has shown an even deeper impact. Clarity of communication also improves what people remember about you and how they feel about you.[12] It makes you feel more familiar to them and makes them trust you more.

If you search the internet for tips on how to effectively communicate, you will come across a range of best practices, many with similar names. At some point, you'll come across "The 7 Cs of Communication: Completeness, Conciseness, Consideration, Clarity, Concreteness, Courtesy, Correctness." Surf a bit more and you'll find "The 5 Cs of Communication: Clarity, Consistency, Creativity, Content, Connections." Keep surfing and you'll be sure to find another "The 5 Cs of Communication," with a slightly different list: "Clear, Concise, Compelling, Curious, Compassionate."

If you kept searching, you'd continue to find more iterations of the same idea. All the lists have valid and useful elements, but they are each suited for different contexts. Communication is always contextual, so taking broad lists and applying them to the interview setting would be a mistake. But, taking the commonalities across the lists and choosing the most applicable does lead to a list of three that are most relevant to you as a candidate:

- Be clear
- Be complete
- Be concise

George Bernard Shaw, author and Nobel Prize winner, famously said, "The single biggest problem in communication is the illusion that it has taken place." What you say and what is heard isn't always the same. There will be times when lack of communication is the interviewer's fault, either because they weren't fully listening or because they misinterpreted something you said. You can't control that. What you can control is your ability to be concise, clear and complete. For interviewing, those are the most relevant Cs of communication.

CHECK FOR UNDERSTANDING

A powerful technique to ensure you are being clear and complete (i.e., have shared all the information needed) is a practice used by great teachers called a "check for understanding." According to research,[13] the technique increases the odds of the recipient learning what you want them to learn. It allows the speaker, in real time, to adjust their answer, clarify, or stay on course.

During an interview this can take several forms. If you provide an answer that is more complex than you'd like or you realize you've started to ramble, pause and ask any one of the following questions to shift the answer back to where it needs to be:

- "I feel like I haven't been as clear as I'd like. Did my answer make sense? Or is there something I can clarify?"
- "I may have given too much detail or gone off-course just now. Can I clarify any of that?"
- "Am I headed in the right direction with this answer? I love this topic and may have talked for too long."

Pausing to make this statement has several positive effects. First, it is a natural way to catch yourself from rambling as you try to make sense in the moment. At some point, we all ramble and it can be difficult to know when we are doing so. Planning in advance to pause and check for understanding minimizes the odds of that going on for too long.

Second, interviewers like candidates who are self-aware. Even if this means showing you are self-aware of a potential misstep. When you acknowledge that you might not have been as clear as you'd like, it won't always prompt the interviewer to say, "That's true . . . I wasn't following you. Can you repeat that?" Sometimes the interviewer has gotten the essence of your answer and just wants to move on. Other times, they haven't gotten the essence, but also just want to move on. Either way, proactively pausing before the interviewer has to interject shows self-awareness and is always appreciated by interviewers.

Another benefit of checking for understanding is that it re-engages the interviewer. If they were starting to mentally wander, you've brought them back. If they wanted to redirect you, it is now easier. If they were frustrated by your rambling or lack of clarity, they would have been even if you didn't pause. At a minimum, they will be glad you paused so they didn't have to figure out how to stop you or redirect you. Communication experts call this a "verbal punctuation" that creates a seam in the conversation and gives them a way back in.

There are two other impacts of this technique. It gives you an opportunity to share a better answer. It is also a chance to make the interview feel more like dialogue. Both play in your favor. Don't hesitate to take control of those moments when you sense you may be lacking clarity. You taking ownership is better than the interviewer owning it. At worst, you'll be in the exact same place. At best, you'll come out ahead.

KNOW YOUR CLOSING

Sometimes candidates continue talking too long because they aren't sure how or where to land. They don't know how to close. You don't have to overthink the solution to this dilemma. You aren't seeking to be the most eloquent speaker. You are potentially talking in lists, using key phrases to make your strengths stand out, creating a three-act structure, or some of each. Keep it simple and complete by closing with one of the following:

End with the third act: If you are using the three-act structure, then remember that the third act is the best and most natural place to end. Whether you end with "results," "benefits," or "now what," just stop there. You may not feel like you are done, but as listeners we all innately know the Hero's Journey is complete.

End with the third point: The "rule of three" is a principle used by writers and content creators because a trio is more effective than any other number. Our innate preference for lists of three predates our modern times. The Latin phrase *"omne trium perfectum"* translates to "everything that comes in threes is perfect," or "every set of three is complete." If you are using a list structure, ending on your third point is a natural way to close.

Use their question to close: Another mental trick is to think of bringing your answer full circle. In other words, close by referencing the question the interviewer asked. It will feel natural and complete to you and the listener if you close with, "And that's an example of feedback I received in my last role."

Use a catch phrase: Sometimes you just need something verbal to trigger your mind to wrap it up. It is almost like a "safe word" you can use to remind yourself to close. Common catch phrases that signal completion are:

- "The bottom line is . . ."
- "To make a long story short . . ."
- "At the end of the day . . ."

Talking too much rarely, if ever, makes things better. If an answer is bad, more talking makes it worse. If an answer is a strong one, talking too much can easily ruin it. Solve this by planning ahead. Predetermining a few mechanisms that will help you close your answer keeps you from over-talking and entering an area of muddled words that is tough to pull yourself out of.

WHAT'S THE PERFECT LENGTH FOR AN ANSWER?

Interviewing is an investment of time that most interviewers don't have. In the early stages of an interview process, you may be interviewed by someone in human resources whose job it is to interview. But if you advance, you will quickly find yourself in front of the staff members and managers you will end up working with. That group doesn't interview as part of their job, and they may or may not enjoy doing it.

One of the things every interviewer dreads is being faced with a candidate who seems to have no idea when to stop talking. Any question asked leads to a one-man show that goes on for a minimum of five minutes. This sometimes happens because the candidate is attempting to do the right thing and be complete. They want to make sure they've covered every base and given all the information needed. But in doing so, they lose the interviewer's attention and their ability to process effectively.

Interviewers don't want to struggle to follow a rambling answer, unsure whether they should be taking notes or if they are wasting their time capturing tangential streams of thought. In addition, if your answers make the interview run over time, you are now cutting into their real job which creates tension and potentially feelings of resentment for intruding even further into their day. The act of interviewing someone, particularly if you have several in a day, can be mentally taxing.

Because of that, you need to make it easy for them to spend time with you. The more concise your answers are, the longer you will hold the attention, respect, and positive feelings of the interviewer. While the previous section gave tips on how to close an answer, you may still be wondering how long your answers should typically be.

The Science and Math Behind the Perfect Length

An important element to know about the human mind is that it is constantly wandering. A study[14] that collected data from over 15 thousand participants in eighty countries found that, on average, our minds wander 47 percent of the time. The range for their findings was from 10 percent to 65 percent. The less effort an activity requires, the more likely the mind will wander during that activity.

A separate study[15] was focused on why the mind wanders in the first place. Dr. Peter Killeen, a psychologist at Arizona State University, and several colleagues were studying attention deficit hyperactivity disorder (ADHD). Their research delved into the physical structure of the brain and they discovered that people with ADHD are on one end of the spectrum, but the underlying physical causes in the brain across the spectrum are the same. The brain's function is based on neurons firing and then accessing energy in the form of glucose or lactate. If neurons don't get access to energy after twelve seconds, they start to get exhausted, your brain begins to lose the ability to pay attention—and it wanders.

The takeaway from both studies isn't that you need to construct a twelve-second answer. Rather, the longer your answer is, the more likely the interviewer is no longer listening. If you give a five-minute answer, they've either missed nearly two and a half minutes of content (47 percent) somewhere along the way, or by the time you've gotten to the important conclusion, they've tuned you out.

From firsthand experience, I know both are exactly what happens during a long answer. When a candidate talks for too long, if my mind doesn't wander aimlessly, it starts to wander specifically. The place it wanders is trying to figure out how to redirect or interrupt the candidate to help them get to the point. Or, it wanders to a negative place where I am no longer judging the content of the answer but the candidate's lack of ability to get to the point.

Under normal circumstances, I either redirect or ask follow-up questions, which is good for the candidate because it allows them to clarify. But when the pattern of long answers continues, I begin to question whether following up will only lead to yet another lengthy answer. Ultimately, time constraints lead to the tactical decision of just moving to the next question.

I also know from having interviewed alongside other interviewers, that candidates can't tell when our minds are wandering. Interviewers know we should be paying attention and often disguise that we aren't. We learn to nod and say "Aha" at the appropriate moments. All of those other decisions interviewers make are at the expense of listening and understanding who you are and what you can do.

So, what is the right length for an answer? Conventional wisdom among interviewers is that a great answer should clock in around *two minutes—three at the most.*

Beyond the science of how the mind wanders, there is also plain, old math.

A typical interview is about an hour long and interviewers usually have about ten questions to ask you. That math leads to six minutes per answer. But you also should calculate about one minute per question asked. Now we are down to fifty minutes total. Most interviewers do about five minutes of preamble and potentially five minutes of time at the end for your questions. Now we are at forty minutes. We still have one more calculation left. For every other question, the interview might have a follow-up question. That question and your answer might take another ninety seconds per question, totaling seven and a half minutes. Now we are at thirty-two and a half minutes left for your answers. Divide that by ten, and we've landed at three and a quarter minutes.

But don't aim for a three-minute answer, shoot for a two-minute answer. Because in the moment, you will likely over-shoot a bit. Aim for the low end and give yourself that little bit of breathing room for the moments when you inevitably will go off-track.

Short Answers

Context, of course, matters. Some questions require very short answers. If the interviewer is just asking a direct factual question, then a thirty-second answer is appropriate:

Interviewer: *Why did you decide to major in biology?*

Candidate: *I had always done well in the sciences. There was a big part of me that wanted to be a doctor. I knew that chemistry and psychology were good degrees to prepare me, but they didn't interest me as much as biology, so I followed what interested me the most.*

These types of questions are fact-based. You aren't trying to hook them with a three-act structure or convince them of a particular skill or relevance of an experience. Those answers are supposed to be short and to the point. Save yourself time for the answers where you are trying to influence.

Be cautious about giving answers that are under thirty seconds. The interviewer is always trying to get a read on the candidate and your interactions with them are the primary source. Candidates who consistently give thirty-second answers, regardless of context, are perceived as uninterested, lacking personality or potentially even hostile. An interview is like any other conversation. If you are consistently short with someone, they will read into it, and their takeaway won't be positive.

HOW YOUR CELL PHONE CAUSES INTERFERENCE

Although I've heard of it happening, I've never had a candidate take a phone call during an interview. Other than a call from a family member with pressing news like a wife in labor, an ill child, or a family member passing away, it's hard to imagine a legitimate reason for taking a call during an interview. Even if those extreme cases don't apply to you, there is still interesting research on cell phones that will make you rethink their impact on your interview.

Silence Your Phone

Before we dive into the science, let's discuss an unforced error no one thinks they will commit—and for that reason, they do. They forget to mute their phone.* Though not nearly as offensive as taking a call during an interview, your phone ringing in the middle of a question is a distraction you don't need. It will distract both you and the interviewer from the experience at hand. It is a forgivable mistake that can be committed by either side.

But as the candidate, you can least afford mistakes of any kind. Particularly when every misstep will still be considered a minor ding against you. The best practice is to write a note to mute your phone on a Post-it and stick it on your phone the night before the interview. The next day, mute your phone in the morning. If your interview is later in the day, leave the Post-it on your phone until you walk out the door and mute it then.

---

* This lands in the category of Interview Basics 101, but the number of times I've interviewed a candidate and been interrupted by their phone ringing warrants these two short paragraphs.

Don't Put It on the Table . . .

It is remarkable how much we are creatures of habit. Taking our cell phone from our pocket and placing it on the table, wherever we are, is a normal social behavior. But during an interview it is an unforced error not worth committing. The first thing to consider is generational. If the person across from you is from the era before cell phones became ubiquitous, a cell phone on the table will seem odd. It will become a distraction taking them away from focusing on you and your answers. But even if the person interviewing you is progressive in terms of social norms or a digital native themselves, science suggests a cell phone in view—or anywhere near you, for that matter—is a problem. Which brings us to the next suggestion.

. . . Actually, Don't Bring It At All

Cell phones have embedded themselves in our lives so deeply that they occupy what's called a "privileged attentional space." This is the same space occupied by things like the sound of your name. Our names mean so much to us that if we are in a conversation and hear our name in someone else's conversation, we are immediately pulled out of our current conversation and become distracted by what is potentially being said in the other conversation.

According to MIT professor Sherry Turkle, cell phones are a reminder that we could be interrupted at any moment.[16] They hold privileged attentional space and therefore, when cell phones are present, we don't give full attention to what we are currently engaged in. Conversations become less engaging and with less depth. This phenomenon has been studied extensively. A study in the *Journal of Social and Personal Relationships* found having a cell phone visible stifled "interpersonal closeness and trust" and kept people from feeling empathy for one another.[17] Two other studies found the "mere presence" of a cell phone diminished task-performance, especially for tasks with greater attentional and cognitive demands.[18] Another study published in *Computers in Human Behavior* indicated that a cell phone's visible presence not only distracted the owner of the cell phone, but others around them who could also see the phone.[19] A study at the University of Texas at Austin found that a cell phone reduces your cognitive capacity even when it is powered off and tucked away in a purse, briefcase, or backpack.[20]

Although these findings are extraordinarily consistent, it sounds extreme that your cell phone, even when off and in your pocket, could negatively impact your performance. It is hard to accept this idea precisely because we are so accustomed to our phones. We can't even imagine them doing that type of harm. So, let's remove the idea of cell phones from this scenario for a moment. If someone simply said to you, "Study after study has shown that if you do X, you will reduce the odds of performing well during an interview." Would you risk doing X?

Obviously, you would not do X. In this case, X is bringing your cell phone to the interview. During an interview, you need every odd in your favor. The solution to all the issues mentioned above is to leave your cell phone in your car. Remove it completely from your being. For some people, this will feel bizarre and they'll feel almost naked. This only highlights the grip the cell phone has on your mind. The odds of any call of actual importance happening during the hour or two you are with your future employer are extremely low.*

Leave your phone in your car. Your performance will be improved. That's worth a missed text from someone about something less important than the interview you are in that will determine your next career step.

---

* The potential exception to this rule is when an organization has a full day of interviews. Depending on your circumstances, being unreachable for an entire day may not be feasible.

SECTION TWO

How to navigate the mind of the interviewer,
so they accurately see your talent.

THE INTERVIEWER'S EGO

If given a choice, do you think people would prefer to feel better about themselves or worse about themselves? There is no twist or trick answer here. No matter how modest we are, no matter our temperament, we all want to feel good about ourselves. Ego—a person's sense of self-esteem or self-importance—is a part of human nature. Furthermore, our egos are influenced by our interactions with others. More specifically, we know from a multitude of studies that a principal way to influence a person's ego is through flattery.

Your first thought may be that you don't respond well to flattery or that flattery doesn't work on you because you quickly associate it with other motives. There is some truth to that reaction, but it is nuanced. Research has shown that flattery intended to serve another purpose isn't as influential as flattery that is sincere. This point of sincerity is important and shouldn't be brushed over.

Studies[1] have shown that people in positions of power can easily tell when someone is ingratiating themselves for personal gain. Not only that, it backfires and loses the person the level of respect they wanted. A study[2] at the University at Buffalo came to a similar conclusion. The researchers found that flattery, when *not* done well can negatively impact inter-personal relationships. The study focused specifically on the workplace in which supervisors who knew a team member was praising them for self-gain rated that person's work performance as lower. However, in both studies, if the compliments were viewed as sincere—then they ranked the person higher.

But research has also identified something counterintuitive about flattery—even when it isn't sincere, it can *still* be influential in a good way. This happens because the negative impact of insincerity doesn't last long while the positive feeling remains.

Two professors at the Hong Kong University of Science and Technology conducted a study[3] in which a new department store contacted people via a mailer that complimented them with phrases such as, "We are contacting you directly because we know you are a fashionable and stylish person." Clearly, this mailer was not hand-crafted for the recipients and the department store had no idea of the receiver's fashion sense. Yet the study found the people who received the flattering mailer had far more favorable feelings toward the store. In the study, there was a negative reaction to the flattery because it was insincere, but that reaction faded. What remained was the affinity they felt for the store.

To demonstrate that ego-enhancement can override questions about sincerity, a different group of researchers[4] used computers to deliver praise. When participants completed a task, the computer would either give generic feedback or sincere praise. The participants were told the sincere praise was based on something they did to receive the praise. When participants felt the computer's praise was based on their input, they left the interaction feeling more positively. There is no way a computer can be sincere. It has no emotion and can neither be sincere or insincere. That didn't matter, the feeling that remained after the interaction mattered more.

This difference between negative, *conscious* feelings and positive, *unconscious* feelings is called "explicit attitudes" versus "implicit attitudes" and is relevant to candidates. The explicit attitudes (negative feelings) tend to fade away. Yet implicit attitudes (positive feelings) continue to positively impact the person flattered. They are affected often without knowing it.* This happens because all humans have a need for self-enhancement. All of us are susceptible to mechanisms that inflate our ego because we innately want to feel good about ourselves. We'll unconsciously hold onto that feeling, even in moments when we aren't 100 percent certain the person delivering it is sincere.

I share this research on sincerity versus insincerity not to suggest you should slather your interviewer with compliments. The risk of it going wrong is too high. Rather, I share it to make clear you have the power to positively influence the interviewer's ego. Especially when done correctly and carefully.

The strategies in this section allow you to make the interviewer feel good about themselves without seeming insincere. The techniques for doing this will be subtle. They are nudges that naturally happen during the course of an interview. What you will learn is how to deliver the feeling without the receiver knowing you delivered it. What will remain beyond the interview is the association between you and that feeling of positive self-enhancement. That association will shift the odds in your favor.

---

* The same experiment found flattery works even more on people who need a bit of energy or positivity. Interviewing isn't easy and can be draining, particularly when doing a series of interviews. Those interviewers are even more primed for flattery.

Flattery in a Group Setting

It is worth mentioning a specific word of caution about influencing ego. Be very careful with flattery when there is more than one decision-maker in the room. Research[5] in the *Journal of Consumer Research* found when people heard someone praising another person, even when sincere, it made them feel envious. The gut reaction is to feel comparison to the person being flattered and to feel some form of negativity toward the person doing the flattering.

If you are being interviewed by two people or a panel, then any flattery you provide should apply to all the interviewers. The following techniques can successfully be adjusted to be directed toward one person or multiple people.

ASK QUESTIONS

The majority of the questions asked during an interview will come from the interviewer. But there is almost always an opportunity to ask the interviewer questions at the end of the interview. There is tremendous power in those moments and since they are fewer, you want to use them strategically and with intention.

Multiple studies have shown that asking questions makes the interviewer feel more engaged and more likely to view you favorably. It also gives you an opportunity to learn whether the job is the right fit for you.[6] But asking questions also provides another benefit—it is one of the most organic ways to flatter an interviewer without being inauthentic.

If the interviewer offers an opportunity for you to learn more by providing time for your questions, you must send the signal that you are interested by using that time. If you do not, even if the interviewer is not visibly bothered, it will be remembered. The signal you have just sent is either a lack of interest or curiosity, or a lack of understanding about how to engage with a decision-maker. In those moments, always ask questions. The key to enhancing their ego is *how* you ask the question.

Elevate Them

Always prepare questions to learn more about the organization or the team you will be joining. These questions will emerge from any reading you do about organization. You may read about a competitor, a comment from the CEO, or a new product. On their website you may be interested in their culture, core values, or strategic direction. There are many areas to choose from. The best approach is to let your curiosity determine what you want to ask. Those questions tend to feel most natural and will therefore land best.

By asking questions, you automatically elevate the interviewer to a higher status. They have information that you want or need. The way you phrase the questions, however, is the secret to amplifying the feeling that comes along with being looked up to.

For example, a common question to ask at the end of a job interview would be:

Candidate: *How would you describe the culture in this organization?*

Asking that question generically is a lost opportunity to elevate the interviewer. The better way to ask the same question would be:

Candidate: *You seem like the right person to ask this question . . . How would you describe the culture in this organization?*

This is the same question, but you've complimented them in a natural way. You've implied that you've identified they can answer this question best. Your question is truthful because any person you talk to in the organization is someone who would be well-suited to share their perspective. But because your phrasing is directed specifically to them, their implicit attitude will shift. Their ego is enhanced and a positive feeling will occur. There are multiple ways to do use this technique.

- "As a person who has achieved success in this organization . . . What advice would you have for someone who also wants to do well here?"

- "I read in your bio that you began your career in sales . . . How has that shaped you as a leader in this organization?"
- "Since you know this role better than I do, what are a few things I should consider that may not be obvious to me?"
- "Based on your experience, what advice do you have for any new person who might join this organization?"
- "I'm interested in learning more about _____. When you were in my shoes, how did you get started?"

With all these questions you are sending specific messages wrapped in a question. "You are successful . . ." "I'm interested in learning from you . . ." "You know things that others don't . . ." "You are special . . ." When you ask someone for advice, you are putting them in a position of knowing more than you, but also in a position of helping you. Both of those are viewed favorably by people. These are not heavy-handed. Most importantly, they deliver a positive feeling associated with you, yet delivered without any question of insincerity.

As you prepare for an interview, write down the questions you truly want to ask. Then rewrite the questions using the various phrases shared above. Find the ones that feel natural coming from you. Depending on your personality, they may initially feel as though you are coming on too strong. But they won't feel that way to the receiver. Even if, in the moment, they briefly feel a lack of sincerity, that will go away and the positive feeling will remain.

They will remember you as someone who was curious about the work. You will be remembered as someone they helped. They will also remember you as someone who made them feel worthy. Those are the kinds of positive memories you want in their mind when they later make a decision about hiring you.

Start with a Question

While asking questions at the end of the interview is most common, the power of asking questions doesn't only work at the end. It also works at the beginning.

As much as we don't want interviews to be a popularity contest, you do want the interviewer to like you. You need as many strategies as possible to tilt the odds toward your candidacy. Asking questions is a natural way to effectively start building likeability with the interviewer. In a study conducted at Harvard, researchers found that people who ask questions were better liked by their conversation partners.[7]

Accomplishing this strategy is not complicated. When you walk into an interview room, you will introduce yourself and exchange a few words of pleasantries. While you are both in that moment—before they shift into interview mode—insert one important type of question.

The question will be simple, genuine, and connected to them as an individual. You don't want to ask, "How are you doing?" That question is generic. You also don't want to make assumptions about the person's interests. For example, people often assume I like sports and will ask a question about a team, athlete, or game. The problem is, I don't watch sports. Although they are trying to build a connection with me, I am now in the awkward position of either saying I am clueless or faking an answer. Neither gets us off to a good start.

Instead, ask one of the following questions:

- "Thanks for taking the time to do this interview. Has your day been full of interviews?"
- "Thanks for this opportunity. I assume your day is filled with interviews?"

They will answer by acknowledging either that their day is full or that it isn't that bad. Regardless of which way they answer, always acknowledge an appreciation for the context you both find yourself in by saying:

- "Well, interviewing isn't always easy, so I appreciate the time we'll have to talk."

You are not simply asking the common question of, "How are you doing?" You are asking a question specific to their condition in the unique context of interviewing. Most importantly, inquiring about a person's condition signals curiosity and care, and your response signals gratitude. The Harvard study showed that this type of dialogue unleashes the special power of questions and makes people feel respected and heard. That's a great way to start a productive conversation that you want to end well for you.

NEVER ASK THESE QUESTIONS

The power of questions can easily cut both ways. Asking questions can give you a competitive edge. Asking the wrong questions can do the exact opposite. If things have been going well during an interview, a minor error won't necessarily change your trajectory. But across the years, there have been many examples I've witnessed of candidates who were doing well, then turned the tide against themselves with questions at the end that threw them off the consideration track.

Those types of stumbles are unforced errors that don't need to happen. Some candidates make the mistake of thinking that because the interviewer has stopped asking questions, the interview is over. Interviewers never stop assessing you. Everything you do is being evaluated. So even when they say, "We're at the end of the interview. Are there some questions I can answer for you?"—they are still evaluating you. Even if they genuinely just want to answer questions that might help you understand the role or the organization, it is impossible for what you do in that moment to not become an input for the decision they must later make.

There are three questions candidates ask that make them lose points from the interviewer's perspective.

"Can you tell me about the salary and benefits?"
This seems like a logical question to ask. After all, an important aspect of any job is how much you'll be paid and how well the organization will support you with benefits. The problem with this question is the timing.

During the interview, you are still convincing them that you are right for the job. Asking about compensation and benefits has two negative effects. First, it sends the signal that you care more about what you will be paid, than the job. The unfortunate truth is that many people take a job for the money. But during the interview, you are still in courtship where they are learning more about you and you are learning more about them. Any questions about compensation destroy that narrative, no matter how truthful they are.

Second, most interviewers won't answer that question. But if they do and you don't like the answer, you are now in an awkward position. You either have to fake that you are satisfied or signal that you hoped for more. The hitch is that you have no leverage at this stage to impact the salary. You don't want to raise the topic of compensation until you know they want to hire you. That way, you can use their desire to hire you to learn what your salary options are.

You will always want to negotiate your salary. Learning about it from the interviewer too soon weakens your position. In their minds, they've now told you and unless you drop out, they'll assume it was in your range. It will seem strange if you get the job and then try to negotiate. This will cause them to think, "But we told this person the salary when they asked, and they never said anything. If they didn't like it, they should have said something then or not wasted our time by staying in the interview process."

Avoid all these misconceptions by not asking about your compensation. Assuming they want to hire you, there will be time to learn more. If they don't hire you, it didn't help to know anyway.

"How did I do in this interview? Is there anything I can re-answer?"

If you do enough research on interviewing, you will find some experts who advise candidates to ask their interviewer how well they performed at the end of the interview. This advice is given because the assumption is it gives the candidate one more chance to sell themselves and provide a rationale for hiring them. Having sat in the interviewer's seat for many years and having sat next to many other interviewers, I can decisively tell you this strategy does not work. It often backfires and has unintended consequences.

First, asking how well you've performed sends signals of insecurity and a need for validation. In psychology this is called approval-seeking behavior and it signals you don't believe you are good enough. If you've done well, the interviewer expects you to know that and asking how you've done sows seeds of uncertainty. Or, it sends a signal that you need constant positive reinforcement. Neither is the perception you want to create.

Second, if you didn't do well, now you've just put the interviewer in an uncomfortable position which no one wants to be in. They either must break bad news to you and say you haven't done well or pretend that you have done well. Neither sits well with interviewers. At best, they'll anchor on the part of the question in which they can give you a second shot at re-answering some questions.

If so, maybe you will provide stronger answers, but the seeds of doubt have already been planted. The idea that you may not have done your best is now in their mind. The impression of you they will remember will not be the candidate who did well but the candidate who wasn't sure of themselves.

If you feel the need to create an opportunity for a final pitch of your skills, don't ask how you did. Instead use the future tense and ask, "Are there any remaining questions that would be helpful for me to answer?" This type of question doesn't put you in a position of inferiority. You aren't suggesting that you've made a flaw. Rather you are suggesting that perhaps more information will be helpful, and you are happy to provide it.

"What is your role here again?"

As mentioned previously, before you go into any interview, you should do as much research about your potential interviewers as possible. Sometimes it is difficult to find out who your interviewers will be. If you do, sometimes it is just as difficult to find a lot of information about them. Earlier in this section, we shared good questions to ask about their perspective and experiences. In doing so, one thing you cannot afford is to send any message that you don't know what they do in the organization. Curiosity about them is a good thing. Being clueless about who they are, is not.

It is dangerous to ask an interviewer what they do because they often assume you know what they do. If they have any level of authority in the organization, they are used to people knowing who they are. By asking them who they are, you are implying they aren't as important as they'd like to believe, or that you haven't done your research. Both are unforced errors that can be avoided by just not asking what their role is. If you don't have any background on the interviewer, don't convey it in a way that breaks a relationship. Jot down their name and you'll get an opportunity to make up for it later when you send a thank-you note.

The opportunity to ask questions in an interview is a gift. Asking the right questions and avoiding the wrong ones is a point of leverage you must take advantage of. The interviewer must remain your focus. They are why you care about this role. They are the person you want to impress. In that moment, they are truly the most important person in the room. Their enhanced sense of self comes from your attention being put on them and it goes away by attention being put on anything else.

LISTENING IS INFLUENCING

Asking questions isn't the only way to enhance someone's ego. Interestingly, the opposite of asking can do the same thing. In the 1950s, two renowned psychologists explored a previously untapped area of influence and along the way, changed the way we think about listening. Dr. Carl Rogers and Dr. Richard Farsons worked at the University of Chicago, and over several decades conducted research together and published numerous studies. The work for which they are most famous was a piece written in 1957 called *Active Listening*.

Although "active listening" is now a commonly used term, it is often misunderstood. People assume it simply means to pay attention while you are listening. But its roots are much more complex and contain lessons for every candidate who wants more control over the outcome of an interview.

Active listening is actually a technique used by therapists to create a change in their client. In this simple sentence is one of the most important elements of active listening. When done properly it *changes* the person being listened to. This is opposite of what most people think. They believe that active listening is about improving your ability to comprehend what is heard. That is true. But it is only half of the power behind active listening.

The other half is that the person being listened to comes away from the conversation different from when they started. This is what makes it different than "passive" listening, in which nothing truly happens. Active listening leads to a set of desired actions that the listener (the candidate) desires in the person they are listening to (the interviewer).

Rogers and Farsons discovered that a specific set of listening techniques changes the person you are listening to. The techniques result in the listener becoming more open to new experiences and more willing to accept another's views. They also become more democratic in their thinking and less authoritarian in their decision-making. In other words, when you use active listening techniques with an interviewer, they are more open to accepting your point of view or the case you are making.

The pair of psychologists found that listening, even passive listening, is never a passive activity. As counterintuitive as it sounds, when you are listening, you are communicating a message to the person talking. When you use active listening practices, you communicate to the interviewer they are worth listening to. You are sending the message that you respect their thoughts and are interested in them. It creates a reciprocal relationship in which, according to Rogers and Farsons, "the one who consistently listens with understanding . . . is the one who eventually is most likely to be listened to."

The following active listening practices are a gold mine for candidates. While the approach was designed for therapists to influence clients, the exact same practices can be used by candidates during an interview.

Summarize the question asked

When the interviewer asks you a question there is as much opportunity to misunderstand as there is to understand. In moments when you aren't completely sure you understand, take control. After the question is asked, briefly summarize the question and repeat it back to the interviewer. This practice ensures you are answering the right question and shows you care about what is being asked.

Ask a clarifying question

Sometimes summarizing the question isn't necessary. When you believe you understand the question but need to do a quick check before potentially going down a wrong path, take control by clarifying. For example, you should say, "Just to clarify, are you asking about my current work experience or what I would hypothetically do in this situation?"

Interviewers don't mind clarifying questions. Most interviewers prefer them because they prefer candidates who require less redirecting or less deciphering afterward. Both techniques—summarizing or clarifying—work because the underlying science has shown that people who ask questions are viewed as good listeners.[8] That type of candidate is appreciated, and that edge makes a difference in the final decision.

Be cautious not to overuse the technique. Use it only when you truly need clarity. If you summarize or ask clarifying questions for the majority of questions, the opposite effect takes hold. You are either viewed as a poor listener or someone who needs to be handheld through every nuance.

Maintain eye contact

When the interviewer is asking you a question, look at them—even if they don't look at you. In Western culture, eye contact is seen as a sign of respect.* In addition, the odds of understanding the question increase when you look directly at the interviewer. Your entire body is a machine for taking in signals and interpreting them. During an interview, your sense of smell, taste, and touch aren't relevant, which leaves the remaining two—sight and sound. You should never remove one of the

---

* There are cultures in which eye contact can be a sign of disrespect. Cultural relativism is important, so be fully aware of the culture in which you are operating to determine whether this advice is appropriate.

primary ways for understanding the world around you by not looking at the person talking to you.

This doesn't mean you need to make unnecessarily long eye contact and create discomfort. Looking away momentarily is natural. But stay face-to-face and keep your attention in the general direction of their face. Your ears are picking up the words and your eyes are picking up a range of other cues that you otherwise wouldn't receive. Your behavior in total is positively impacting the interviewer's self-esteem.

Don't jump to the end of the question

Let's remove ourselves from the interview table for a moment. We have all had the experience in which we are talking to someone and they keep finishing our sentences before we complete them. Most people get annoyed by that. Especially if the other person finishes it incorrectly. Similarly, we each have been the person listening to someone and simultaneously preparing a response before they have completed their point.

Active listening requires you to make neither of these mistakes. Don't assume you know where the interviewer is headed with their question. Don't load your own response while listening. This advice is critical during an interview because, when not followed, the damage is worse than an annoyed friend. When a candidate thinks they know where the question is headed, they often stop listening and start loading their answer. When they finally do answer, it is to a different question than what was asked. This mistake can come from a good place because they've prepared well and are already selecting from the range of examples they will provide.

But it is still a huge mistake. It makes no difference how great your answer is, if you don't answer the question asked. Some interviewers will redirect you, but your credibility will take a hit. Other interviewers have less patience or time and simply move on. They will mark the answer as wrong even though they know it was a mistake of hearing, not a mistake of knowledge or skill.

To avoid this train yourself to do two simple things:

- Stay completely in the moment with the question, until the very last word of the sentence.
- Pause for a moment after the question is asked.

Staying in the moment is essential because as soon as you leave the moment, you risk missing part of the question and therefore part of the answer. The pause is important because that is when you need to do your thinking. Unfortunately, most candidates have bought into the myth that the ability to quickly answer a question is a sign of intelligence. Even more troublesome is that many interviewers believe the same myth. However, a slight pause has also shown to be an equally strong indicator of intelligence because it signals thoughtfulness.

If you don't buy into the myth of quick answers, the interviewer won't either. Take a few seconds to think. You can also say, "Give me a second to think about that." Doing either makes the interviewer feel like what they've said is worth reflection. It is a subtle sign of respect and heightened value you place on their words.

STRATEGIC GRATITUDE

You should always send a thank-you note after the interview. Some people send a thank-you note via email, others send a handwritten note. You should not only do both, you should also strategically time them.

Sending a note via email does not have the same effect as a handwritten note. Emails in today's culture are transitory. They don't hold a particular place in anyone's mind. They often represent more work for the interviewer because they raise the question about whether they should reply, and with what response.

But the value of sending a thank-you email is that you can send it shortly after the interview, and that outweighs the downside. I recommend sending it by the end of the same day you interviewed. Depending on when they are discussing your candidacy, sending a thank-you email by the end of the day signals you had the interviewers top of mind and puts you top of mind for them. They will appreciate this attention and that could be a nudge that helps you.

Do not send everyone the same note. Include something specific to your interview with them—a specific comment made, a commonality shared, etc. When an interviewer gets an email, sometimes they forward it to other team members that also interviewed you. If you send the same email to each of them, it will lack sincerity. If you customize each email, however, they likely won't share it because they will know it was meant for them specifically. And if they do, it will be clear you customized for each person. While some people may view a thank-you note sent to everyone less favorably, they will at least know it was meant specifically for them—which causes them to hold onto the positive feeling.

After you've sent the email, send the handwritten note the next day. The competitive advantage comes from doing both. This is valuable for several reasons. First, handwritten notes clearly take more time than an email. The fact that you've taken the time to write a note sends another message about your investment in them.

Second, it makes you stand out because most people don't write handwritten notes because it seems old-fashioned. But that only helps your odds because it makes you stand out. No one is ever turned off by a handwritten note. They may quickly read it and toss it in the trash. But for a moment, they have an appreciation for you and that shifts their implicit attitude positively.

Third, sending an email followed by a written note is a one-two punch. The email lands with them immediately, in case they are making quick decisions. The written note arrives a few days later. If they are still seeing candidates, you've just put yourself top of mind again. This is where you want to be.

Always invest in a quick email, customized. Then always send a follow-up handwritten note, also customized. All those little nudges add up. You've literally delivered the positive feeling that draws people toward you. When it comes to landing the job you want, that's the direction you want your interviewers to lean.

FAMILIARITY

You face a unique type of pressure when you walk into the interview room. The interaction you are about to have will determine whether you get the job you want; the person across the table seems to hold the cards and you aren't sure what cards they will play. This book is about helping you understand that you also hold cards. It teaches you how to play those cards based on a better understanding of how interviewers think and make decisions.

In many ways, their experience is a mirror image of yours. One similarity is you are both under pressure. While you operate under the pressure of making decisions that will land you the right job, they have to make decisions that will land them the right person. Researchers have spent a lot of time studying decision-making under pressure. What they've learned provides insight you can use to your benefit.

Let's start with a group of psychologists at Stanford University who ran a unique experiment that shed light on how the brain operates. In the experiment, the researchers had participants attempt to solve a complicated word puzzle with the promise of winning money if they were successful. They found that when people make decisions under pressure, they are subject to a powerful cognitive bias called the "familiarity heuristic."

To measure the effect of pressure, some participants were given as much time as they needed to solve the puzzle, while others were only given four minutes. All of them were then given the option of choosing a long puzzle or a short puzzle. The only other information they were told was that the shorter puzzle was created by a stranger and the longer puzzle was created by someone they knew. The identity of that person was never revealed, because it wasn't true. The researchers simply wanted the participants to believe the puzzle was built by someone familiar to them.

All available evidence in this experiment suggested the participants under a time constraint should pick the shorter puzzle because that would increase the odds of them winning the money. As you would expect, the participants who were not under pressure chose the shorter puzzle. But the participants under the pressure of time, did the opposite. Incredibly, those participants more often chose the longer puzzle which they believed was created by someone familiar to them.

The preference for familiarity has been studied across a range of contexts and cultures. In every iteration its power is significant. A study[9] published in the *Japanese Journal of Psychology* showed participants a set of symbols from the Japanese alphabet. The duration of the exposure was very short, as low as thirty milliseconds in some cases. This level of exposure was such that the symbols were not consciously registered by the participants and they could not recall seeing the letters. Despite this, when the participants were later shown two different sets of alphabets, they liked the set they had previously been exposed to. They couldn't recall seeing the set, but it felt familiar, which resulted in it being favored.

In yet another context, researchers studied the effect of familiarity on people's investment decisions. Similar to interviews, investments contain uncertainty and risk. Under those conditions, researchers Chip Heath and Amos Tversky found[10] when people had to choose between multiple gambles to make, they chose the one that was more familiar to them—even if the odds of losing were higher. Separately, Columbia professor Gur Huberman found[11] that people invested in stocks whose names they were familiar with. Regardless of the stock's performance and the knowledge that a diversified portfolio was a better investment, familiarity reigned supreme and drove people's decisions.

Clearly, decision-making is deeply impacted by familiarity. When we think something is familiar to us, we make decisions in favor of that thing. "Familiarity" equals "safety" in people's subconscious. We are attracted to people who seem familiar because they seem less likely to cause us harm. Familiarity means we have been previously exposed to something, and we survived it, therefore our brain steers us toward it. That is exactly what you want to create in the interviewer's mind.

Hiring decisions that interviewers make are filled with pressure and uncertainty. There is real risk in making a mistake. When interviewers are assessing a candidate, on the surface they are looking for skills and attributes. But subconsciously, they want safety. They want to know you won't screw things up and make them look bad. Your answers are a big part of that equation. But interviewers often make decisions based on their gut. You want them to trust their gut feelings about you. To do so, you need to use the power of familiarity. Simply put, you need to seem familiar to them.

FAMILIAR BY ASSOCIATION

A technique that strong interviewers use to build rapport with you is to find a point of commonality on your resume and mention it at the start of the interview. Perhaps they went to the same school or worked in the same city as you. Interviewers will casually bring this up at the start because it builds trust between you and the interviewer. That trust is what the interviewer wants because they want you to feel comfortable revealing as much information about yourself as possible.

Your interviewers may not take this approach. If they don't, you always should. You want to find a point of commonality to increase their feeling of trust, and just as importantly, their familiarity with you.

To accomplish this, try to find out in advance who you will be interviewing with and do research on them. The names of your interviewers aren't always provided up front. So, you may have to take an additional step and ask whoever is managing the hiring process to share who the interviewers will be. It is rare for them to not want to share this information. After all, you will meet them anyway. Even if they don't share the information, it doesn't hurt to ask.

Assuming you find out who they are, search the internet for them. With the advent of social media, you will likely find genuine points of commonality that spark the feeling of familiarity. Did you study the same major or work in the same city? Do you have the same hobby? Support the same causes or teams? Do you share any friends or acquaintances on LinkedIn? Did you hold similar positions at some point in your careers? Try to find areas that allow you to bridge the gap of unfamiliarity with the interviewer. As you exchange the normal initial greetings, mention the item you uncovered:

> Candidate: *Great to meet you, Hannah. Thanks for taking the time to interview me. I noticed on LinkedIn that you worked in Los Angeles. I went to undergrad there. What part of town did you work in?*

This type of approach allows you to find a point of commonality. By taking charge of it, you can drive toward something familiar. The above comment allows you to mention places you know that may be familiar to the interviewer, thereby making yourself familiar by association.

When using this approach, primarily draw on professional experiences or career-related points of overlap. Those feel less intrusive than referring to very personal experiences. This can be a fine line, but in general, referencing hobbies, sports, or even a friend in common won't seem odd. But referencing their family members (siblings, children, etc.) should be avoided.

While employers and employees alike are increasingly using social media to learn about each other, you don't want to raise alarms about privacy. If you have doubts about whether you should highlight a commonality—then don't. There are many other strategies at your disposal and you don't want to risk hurting your odds in an attempt to improve them.

SOCIAL MEDIA AND FAMILIARITY

If your interviewer has a social media presence, it can be a mechanism for learning about them, so you don't go into any conversation blind. The things they post, repost, or like will tell you about their interests, views, and beliefs. That is valuable information because it can help you build familiarity. But you should be cautious using social media for anything beyond quietly gathering intel.

When to Connect with an Interviewer through Social Media

The social media platform and the privacy settings will determine how much insight you can actually learn about your interviewers. If the person is on a platform where you need to request to be friends or to connect—*do not* make that request before the interview.

Everyone has different levels of comfort about requests from strangers. Because you aren't familiar to the interviewer yet, trying to connect via social media can feel out of place. Since they don't know your motive, doubt can be triggered and they won't be sure if they should accept.

As a candidate, you don't want your interviewer to spend any mental energy on those concerns. So, prior to meeting an interviewer, do not send any invite requests via social media. After you interview, however, you should connect via social media. Since you are now a little more familiar to them, you simply send the request to connect, with a short note if the platform allows it:

> "It was great to meet you. Whichever way this interview process turns out, I look forward to staying connected."

With this type of request, you aren't implying any expectation of an outcome nor are you requesting an action. It is just a genuine desire to remain connected. Assuming they accept, you now have a foot in the door to learn what matters to them and how those things genuinely overlap with what matters to you. In future interviews, those items can come up naturally to reinforce the feelings of familiarity. If you both love sports, you now know you can reference a recent game the next time you meet. If you are both food lovers, that's another point of connection that can be referenced to increase familiarity.

The opportunity to build familiarity may not always happen right at the start, but never lose sight of it as a strategy you can continue to implement throughout your interactions with anyone who will have input on the hiring decision.

Twitter

There is one exception to the rule about not connecting with an interviewer before the interview. That exception is Twitter. On Twitter, most people's profiles are public and you can follow someone without having to make a request. It won't seem strange if a candidate follows an interviewer on Twitter. It indicates they are interested in the interviewer's thoughts and reactions to the world.

Before you follow them though, see what content they post. If it is very political, very personal, or controversial in any other way, then you should *not* follow the person. They will notice that you followed and may assume you agree with their views. Whether you do or not, you shouldn't cross that line at that point. But if the person is posting their general opinion, anecdotes, retweeting, etc. then you should follow them.

The reason you are following them isn't just because you want to get familiar *with them*. You are also doing it so when you arrive for the interview, you feel familiar *to them*. Most people don't have an enormous number of Twitter followers and are flattered when someone follows them. When you follow an interviewer, they will notice and will then look at your profile.* They may or may not follow back, but that doesn't matter. What matters is that this brief interaction falls directly into the research on the mere exposure effect.

When they do meet you, you won't seem entirely new to them, even if they don't recall much from your profile. That pre-exposure will automatically make them predisposed to feel familiarity and therefore, safety and positivity toward you. That's all you want, an edge that will come into play later when your name is being discussed.

LinkedIn

As mentioned, asking to connect with an interviewer prior to interviewing is risky. That has happened to me on multiple occasions and it usually isn't a great strategy. When I receive an invite from someone that I'm about to interview, it puts me in a tough spot. I either need to accept, but then worry that if we don't advance them, I've sent the wrong signal somehow. Or ignore them, but that also sends a signal that is potentially awkward when they show up for the interview.

But a few candidates have done this in a way that isn't awkward and does work in their favor. Those candidates sent a request to connect before the interview, but they included a note calling out the intention. The note read:

"I'll be interviewing with you in a few days. Connecting at this point can be awkward since we don't know what

---

* It goes without saying your own online presence shouldn't turn off a potential employer. This book isn't focused on that aspect. A quick internet search will provide an abundance of advice on managing your online presence.

the future holds. No pressure to accept. My hope is we can stay in touch, regardless of the interview outcome."

I felt like they were smart to network in this way. Most importantly, when I did meet them in person, they felt familiar. I had glanced at their LinkedIn profile, not because I had to, rather because I was curious about who would send this invite. Their note added some "voice" to the content. These are all positive emotions. I felt I knew them just a bit more than other candidates. That feeling shifted me toward them enough to make a difference if there was a tough decision to make.

HOW TO SOUND FAMILIAR

One of the difficulties when joining a new job is learning a new language. Each organization—sometimes each role—has its own lingo, acronyms, and catchphrases that are used among co-workers. A new person on the job has to learn that language. The same can happen during an interview, but with a twist. You will often enter a job interview with *your* own lingo and language from a previous role. That language may be foreign to your interviewer. If you use that language with them, you may not only make it harder for them to follow you, you will seem unfamiliar to them.

If you are in similar industries, that can make it easier and there will be less concern about a language barrier. But if you are not, then there are two steps you must take. First, lose the jargon and vernacular from your previous role. Second, return to the earlier chapter on custom-building your resume and revisit all the advice provided there. Those words they use in the job description or across the website to describe the desired skills and "how" the job is to be done are words you want to absorb. Along the same lines, recall they may have words that convey their organizational culture, values, and beliefs. Knowing those words means there will be less translation and allows you to use language familiar to them.

You may be concerned this could backfire or make you seem inauthentic. It won't. I've been on the receiving end of this tactic. There have been moments when someone I've interviewed has used language so close to language our organization uses that I've afterward said to others, "They must have studied our website." But that comment wasn't based on a negative concern. It was just an observation that clearly this person did their homework. It didn't change the fact that I had found myself nodding at many things they were saying during the interview.

Most people won't consciously notice when you use this strategy. If they do, it won't hurt you. Most people will be impacted subconsciously. They will find themselves leaning toward you and they will credit that to the answers, traits, and skills you share about yourself.

SECTION THREE

*Turning the lens inward to focus on maximizing
your nonverbal signals, emotions, and thought processes.*

IMPRESSION MANAGEMENT

During an interview, so much of what the interviewer believes about you comes from what you say. But it would be a mistake to think your words are the only things that influence them. This section primarily provides practices that leverage the power of nonverbal influence. These practices allow you to influence the interviewer without ever saying a word. Nonverbal influence falls into a broader category of social psychology called "impression management."

Impression management is how an individual maintains, defends, creates, and/or enhances their identity. It refers to the process by which we control the impressions others have of us because those impressions will be how they evaluate and treat us.[1] Sociologist Erving Goffman is credited with conceptualizing and studying this topic extensively. Two of his key ideas are particularly relevant to candidates: (a) how you present yourself sets the tone and direction of interactions, and (b) we can manage impressions others have of us.

As a professional, you likely aren't surprised by these ideas and understand their importance in the workplace. The understanding of how to *intentionally* use impression management, however, is what separates those who get hired into the workplace from those who don't. Missteps in impression management are often due to unforced errors. You may find some of the strategies in this section address mistakes you believe you would never make. That is a dangerous assumption and part of the reason why people commit unforced errors. No one thinks they are going to hit the ball into the net or outside the lines. But they do. In the same way, no one thinks they have poor body language, will arrive late, or won't dress appropriately.

But candidates consistently and unintentionally commit these errors. We've all been late somewhere. We've all arrived at a function and realized we weren't dressed at the appropriate level. We've all caught ourselves slouching. Every one of those things sends a loud message, without a word ever being said. Believing you won't make any of these unforced errors isn't enough to stop them from happening. Professor Caroline F. Keating, a psychologist whose work focuses on leadership, social dominance, and nonverbal communication, has found that there is no neutral gear with nonverbal influence—you are either intentionally moving forward or you will find yourself in reverse.[2]

Unforced nonverbal errors are going to put you in reverse if you don't prepare for them. The strategies in the following chapters put you in control of the things you think won't happen, but always do. They allow you to move forward when others won't.

THE TRUTH ABOUT BODY LANGUAGE

The moment you step into the interview room, the interviewer is beginning to form their opinion. The first thing the interviewer will notice is your physical appearance. The machinery of the interviewer's mind begins turning and logic is once again at the wheel, driving decisions. The logic in this case is the belief that if you appear confident and competent, then you are confident and competent. The amount of time you have to influence the direction of that opinion is limited.

There is no shortage of articles entitled, "Twelve Secrets of Body Language," or "Eight Ways Your Body Language Conveys Confidence," or "The Thirty-Two Secrets of Body Language." The problem is, when you go into an interview you can't juggle thirty-two, or even eight things to manage your body language. Furthermore, most of the items on those lists aren't relevant for the interview setting. For example, there is evidence that standing with your feet apart and firmly planted displays confidence. But crossing your legs as you stand or keeping your feet close together signals timidity. While that's great to know, it only helps if you plan on standing during the entire interview.

Beyond the articles, the research on impression management is also plentiful. Almost too plentiful. Studies have found that women are better at producing facial expressions that are interpreted correctly by the viewer.[3] But other than positive facial cues such as smiling and nodding, can men learn to make those expressions? Discoveries have also been made about the pros and cons of eyebrow raising. Should you now practice controlling your eyebrows? Many researchers have examined the use of touch to influence others. Perhaps finding ways to

125

touch the interviewer without seeming inappropriate would be worth learning? At some point the ideas become too complex and are no longer actionable.

However, if you look across the wide body of research on body language for elements that are relevant for candidates, you will emerge with two strategies that are actionable and backed by science. Each of them has practices associated with it that will lead to you being viewed as confident and competent.

Expansive Body

Dr. Judee K. Burgoon is a professor of Communications Family Studies and Human Development at the University of Arizona. She is the director of research as well as the director of human communication research for the Center for the Management of Information. She has been studying nonverbal communication for nearly five decades and is widely recognized as a top scholar in communication.

Burgoon's research is the foundation for much of what is cited in the field of body language as it relates to confidence. Her findings show that confident people tend to present them-selves in more "open" body positions. Their arms are held out slightly farther and they use more expansive gestures. They literally take up more space. Less confident people do the oppo-site. Rather than open body position, they are defensive and contract themselves to take up less space. They sit with arms and legs held closer and use very little, if any, gestures.[4]

A lot of Burgoon's work was made famous by Amy Cuddy, a Harvard Business School professor who gave a TED Talk on benefits of "power posing" and how it creates the perception of confidence. Her work suggests that small tweaks to your body language can produce tangible improvements in the moment. For example, she suggests the Wonder Woman pose—feet planted squarely apart, hands on hips, chin up. That may sound dramatic, but research has shown that a person who holds their arms akimbo is viewed as more confident.

Other poses Cuddy suggests are used when closing a deal (hands on table, leaning forward) or pitching an idea (hands clasped behind head, leaning back). As much as body language matters, you likely won't strike either of those poses during an interview, nor will you saunter in like Wonder Woman. So how can you use what Burgoon and Cuddy have both found to be successful?

An important finding from their research is that body language doesn't only send the signal of confidence and competence to the interviewer, it also sends that message to yourself. You don't want to just look confident—you want to feel confident as well. This means you should use overly expansive body language as a *preparation technique.*

Victory Before the Fight

The first technique to use is done shortly before the interview. Find a moment for yourself where you can stand, maybe in the parking lot, the restroom, or a break room where you are alone. Stretch your arms over your head as if you are celebrating a victory. Pump your fists into the air as though you have already accomplished something great. Cuddy suggests doing this for two minutes to get the necessary hormonal changes. In practice, that can feel like a long time. If you were celebrating a real-life victory, you wouldn't do it for two minutes, you would do it for thirty seconds or so. I recommend doing two to three sets of thirty seconds each. If you are in a public place and it looks awkward, don't pump your fists, just do an upward stretch for the same effect.

The movement alone will expand your body. The trick is to hold on to that bit of expansion as you head into the interview. Staying in a more upright and full position continues to send the signal of confidence and competence to yourself and to the interviewer as you greet them.

Two-Shooter

Finding the movement that feels right to you is important. It's also important to be realistic about whether you are in a place where you can pump your fists in the air or do a dramatic upward stretch. If you need a movement that garners less attention but has the same effect, then try the "Two-Shooter."

Stand with your arms hanging at your sides. Then bend them halfway at the elbow as though you are a cowboy with two pistols in your hand, each finger pointing directly forward. Keep your elbows in at your side and rotate just your hands, so your palms are now open and face up. You should now be standing with your elbows bent at 90-degree angles with your palms up, as if you are offering a prayer. Now, *keeping your arms bent, elbows at your side and palms facing up*, rotate your arms so your thumbs are pointing behind you. Once you've gone as far as you can, drop your arms at your side.

This movement pulls your shoulders back and pushes your chest out. You may feel as though your chest is puffed out too far. If so, just bring it in a bit. But maintain this feeling of fullness, of taking up a little more space as you enter the interview room. You'll eventually return to your normal posture, but that boost mentally benefits you and shapes the interviewer's initial impression.

Still Skeptical?

If you are skeptical of either technique, consider one other surprising piece of science that supports the practice of expanding your body. Researchers from the University of British Columbia found that expansion, specifically raising your hands, is innate to human behavior.[5] It is how our minds and bodies are engineered.

They studied the body language of Olympic and Paralympic athletes who were sighted and those who were blind. Both the sighted and the blind athletes showed the same expansive body language—even to the point of throwing their arms in the air when succeeding. This included athletes who were *blind since birth* and had never seen others do this movement. This was not a behavior they were mimicking. It is a behavior coded inside of us.

That is what you are using to your advantage. You are sending a signal both to yourself and to the interviewer that you are succeeding. You are aware of it consciously, but its effect on you and the interviewer is much deeper.

Gestures

Burgoon's research also emphasized the importance of using hand gestures to signify confidence and competence. Gestures are one of the most basic and innate forms of communication. All of us learn to gesture before we learn to speak. As early as eight months, children begin to draw attention or point to objects or events. Between nine and twelve months, children start making requests with their hands such as reaching for an object with an open-and-closed grasping motion.

Gestures help others understand what we mean and make us more accessible to the person we are communicating with. According to Susan Goldin-Meadow, a professor of psychology at the University of Chicago, gestures have been shown to accelerate learning and help us with our recollection of memories as we are talking. Both of which are helpful to interviewer and candidate alike.

Gestures to Avoid

Not using your hands at all can be perceived as a sign of indifference. You never want the interviewer to think you aren't interested in them or the organization. Even if you aren't a big user of your hands while talking, don't just keep them in your lap. Use them a little. Similarly, don't have your hands in your pockets as you enter a room. It can be perceived as too casual, more importantly, research has shown that hidden hands make you seem less trustworthy.

Gestures to Consider

I don't recommend trying to memorize and then utilize all the different signals that your hands can send. Rather, raise your awareness of the three most studied hand gestures:

- Hands open and facing upward: *This signals that your being honest and are open to ideas. They are a welcoming gesture.*
- Hands open and facing each other, with your fingers pointing toward the interviewer: *This signals that you have expertise in the topic being discussed. They connotate a preciseness and specificity to your thinking.*
- Hands open and palms down: *This signals that you are certain about the topic you are discussing. You don't have any doubts about the point you are making. You are reassuring them of the facts you are sharing.*

Trying to memorize what to do when isn't the point. Rather, determine the value you want to signal the most—honesty, expertise, or confidence—and primarily use that gesture. If you don't have a preference, then don't overthink it and skip this set of gestures.

Stay in the Box

While research often mentions expansive gestures as signals of confidence, there is the danger of gesturing too wildly. If you gesture too big you will be perceived as out of control. The way to maximize your hand gestures without overdoing it is to remember to keep your hands "within the box."

In other words, when making a point, think of a box which has the top of your chest as the top, your waist as the bottom and your shoulders as the sides. Keep your gestures inside that box and you will convey confidence without appearing scattered.

Authenticity

If any of the practices in this section feel as though they are inauthentic or too structured, that is a normal reaction. The belief that we shouldn't have to change who we are to get a job is a valid one. Stay true to who you are. But the tactics mentioned here aren't about changing who you are. They are about improving your ability to communicate who you are.

You don't want the interviewer to write you off before you even get a chance to express what you can do and how you are a fit for the role. One way or another, your body language will convey a message, so be thoughtful about the message. Use the practices to take control and make it your message.

More importantly, keep in mind the research indicates that shifting your body language is as much about how you see yourself as how others see you. Studies[6] have found that candidates who sat more upright reported higher self-esteem and a better mood than those who slouched. Candidates with more open body language reported that they felt excited, strong, and enthusiastic. Those with more closed body language felt the opposite—nervous, passive, sluggish, and even fearful.

If you struggle with the idea of impression management for the interviewer's sake, then at least do it for what you are impressing upon yourself.

YOUR CLOTHES CHANGE HOW THEY THINK

Mark Twain once wrote, "Clothes make the man. Naked people have little or no influence on society." The fact that what you wear affects how you are perceived is a long-known truth dating even further back than the Twain's comment. Four hundred years ago, a Catholic priest named Desiderius Erasmus Roterodamus coined the phrase, "*vestis virum facit*" which translates to, "clothes make the man."

While you will never show up for an interview naked, research suggests you may show up dressed in a way that hurts the odds of you landing the job you want. A CareerBuilder survey of 2,765 employers found that 41 percent were more likely to promote employees with professional attire and a third of employers will send an employee home for dressing inappropriately. If those rules apply once you are hired, they are certain to affect how you are perceived while you are being hired.

Casual dress codes are increasingly common, but candidates often make the mistake of thinking that also applies to the interview. You need to look no further than any list of "Top Ten Mistakes Candidates Make," and you'll find "dressing inappropriately." Whether it's Glassdoor, TopInterview, Monster.com, or Forbes—every single one cites the clothes you wear as a determining factor of whether you land a job.

When you are strategic about what you wear, you are using the psychology of impression management to your advantage. A study found that when you dress well, the prevailing perception isn't simply that you are well-dressed. The study found when you are dressed well, others perceive you as more confident, successful, flexible, and a higher earner.[7] Other studies have found that being better dressed leads to the perception that you are more intelligent.[8] Another found that a person in uniform is more likely to have others follow their commands. With that type of science firmly in mind, you have one of two choices. Either use the science in your favor. Or let it be used against you.

Believing your personality or competence will overcome mistakes in how you dress is a major unforced error. Some people feel that being judged for what you wear is superficial and, in the name of authenticity, they resist adjusting their appearance. But judgment is a part of human nature. Not acknowledging how that influences decision-makers actually paints you as the one with poor judgment. Dressing a specific way isn't about conforming to other people's norms, it is about strategically making other people think what you want them to think.

The Three Rule Dress Code

The rules for how to dress during an interview are not complex. There are three things to remember. First, do some research. Find out what the dress code is for the team you are interviewing with. If you don't know anyone who works at the organization then do the next best thing—call the person who is coordinating your interview and ask what the dress code is. If you don't feel comfortable doing that, call the office anonymously. Whoever answers, simply tell them, "I'm interviewing there in a few weeks, can you tell me how people normally dress in the office?"

This may sound awkward, but everyone has been in the shoes of the candidate who isn't sure what to wear. The odds are in your favor that the person on the line will give you an honest answer that will help you tremendously.

Once you've done the reconnaissance, the second rule is simple—dress one notch above how people in the office normally dress. If they are a T-shirt and jeans organization, then wear jeans and T-shirt and blazer. Or wear jeans and a polo shirt. If they mostly wear khakis and a polo, throw on a blazer. If they wear a suit and tie, then wear a suit and tie as well. (This is the one place where you don't want to dress one notch above. No one wants to see you in a top hat.)

Many businesses have a website that features their staff. Use their website to determine how they dress. Look at the people in the pictures and dress like the person who is either middle or most well-dressed in the images.

The third rule is also simple. You want people to remember you and not be distracted. Keep it simple. Don't wear cologne or perfume. Don't over-accessorize. Keep jewelry to a minimum. Some candidates truly feel they must have freedom of expression and want to interview as who they are. If your identity is so closely tied to your clothes that you won't change, then don't change. Otherwise, recognize there are many ways to express your identity other than your clothes. If you want to work in the organization you're interviewing with, you'll have to adjust to the context in which you will be operating, starting with the interview.

Expression of your authentic self is important for you to consider when determining whether you'll fit into the organization. The advice in this book does not apply to anything that represents your heritage or culture. As an example, a common concern—for women in particular—is whether they can wear their hair in a way that is customary to their race, ethnicity, or culture. My recommendation is if you have to hide something integral to your identity as a person, don't hide it. We all need to make adjustments in work environments. Shifting your attire is understandable. Denying your culture is not.

If you decide it is a place you want to be, then getting the job offer requires being strategic. Even if the company you're interviewing with is very progressive, the person doing the interview is still making snap decisions and anything that distracts them will hurt you. Keep it simple during the interview. Once you've got the job and have a better understanding of the work culture, then make decisions about how you want to express yourself through your clothing and accessories.

YOUR CLOTHES CHANGE HOW YOU THINK

In psychology, the term "abstract thinking" refers to a type of cognitive functioning relevant to performing well in an interview. To think in an abstract manner means to think beyond what is simply in front of you—it involves more complex thoughts. Abstract thinking takes what is concrete and allows you to conceptualize new ideas. It helps you explain relationships and draw conclusions that go beyond what is obvious to others. With abstract thinking, you can take what is learned in one context and transfer it to another. It strengthens your ability to reflect on ideas and experiences and see how they relate to and influence one another.

During an interview, you will often be asked questions that require you to be in reflective state of mind. You will be expected to answer questions based on less information than you'd normally be presented with. To succeed you will need to step beyond normal thought processes and provide an answer that is coherent, yet more sophisticated than answers other candidates might provide.

Abstract thinking is central to answering interview questions and there isn't a "secret" way to turn it on. But as we've learned by now, to succeed during an interview you need strategies that actively give you control, and those that help you get out of your own way. A strategy to improve your abstract thinking falls into this second category and getting out of your own way goes back to how you dress.

Perception of Self

Getting others to believe what you know about yourself is only half the battle. The other half is getting *you* to believe in yourself. What you wear plays a role in that. As much as your appearance impacts what others think about you, the truly incredible power of dressing the part is what it makes you think about yourself and even *how* it makes you think.

A group of scientists from California State University, Northridge and Columbia University found that the clothes we wear influence our ability to engage in abstract thinking.[9] More specifically, they found that the more formal your clothing, the better your ability to engage in that type of thinking. According to the researchers, "The formality of clothing might not only influence the way others perceive a person, and how people perceive themselves, but could influence decision-making in important ways through its influence on processing style." What stands out in their study is that even when the researchers controlled other factors that could influence outcomes, such as socio-economic status, the positive impact of formal clothing still held firm.

In a separate study[10] done at the Kellogg School of Management at Northwestern University, a concept known as "enclothed cognition" was developed. The experiments were designed to see the effect of the symbolic meaning of clothes. In a series of experiments, subjects were asked to perform tasks and were either given a white doctor's coat or a "regular" coat described to the participants as a painter's coat. In all cases, the coat was exactly the same. The only thing that changed was what people thought about the coat. Because of what we associate with doctors and the formality of that profession, when subjects wore what they were told was a doctor's coat, they made less errors on tests of their attention and were able to maintain heightened attention for longer.

Cognitive science consistently supports the phenomenon that the type of clothing you wear puts you into a different psychological state. When you apply this to your next interview, keep in mind that "formal" is contextual. The rule about dressing one notch above the organization's norm continues to be important here.

If everyone in the organization wears jeans and sneakers, you should not show up in a suit and tie. That would be counterproductive. But by dressing one notch above (jeans, sneakers, and a blazer) you will feel a bit more formal. This shift in clothing will positively impact your own internal state—closer attention to detail, more sustained attention, an improved ability to learn from experience, make inferences, and form judgments—which will impact your ability to do well in the interview.

If you couple those improvements with improved perception by others, then you've just found a mechanism for tilting the odds toward you with little more than a strategic choice about what to wear.

SHAPING THE INTERVIEWER'S MEMORY

What an interviewer learns about you goes beyond their immediate experience with you. It is also determined by their *memory* of that experience. In ordinary circumstances, there are many things that influence how we remember an event. Fortunately, interviews occur in a more controlled environment and there is far less occurring to shape their memory. That is an advantage because it allows you to focus on two ways that the interviewer's mind works—with them you have the power to create memories that work in your favor.

Cortisol versus Oxytocin (Don't Be Negative)

A straightforward strategy to creating the memory you want is to simply avoid coming across as negative—even when describing a difficult situation. Research has shown that negative and positive language have a different effect on the listener's brain.[11] Negative comments cause the listener to produce higher levels of cortisol. That hormone shifts the brain toward conflict aversion and away from thinking and active listening. Negative comments literally make it harder for the interviewer to listen to you.

Positivity on the other hand, has the opposite effect. The chemical reaction that occurs due to positivity is the production of oxytocin. This hormone increases the listener's ability to collaborate, communicate, and trust the person they are communicating with. Those are the exact feelings you want to generate. When the interview is over, that is the memory you want them to have of you.

It's worth noting that the cortisol created by negativity lasts longer than the oxytocin created by positivity. The effect of heightened cortisol can last a full day and impact future behavior. Oxytocin metabolizes more quickly, and its effect is not as long-lasting.

This means the strategy is not just to be positive. That result is not as long-lasting. The additional step to improve the interviewer's memory of you is to intentionally avoid specific elements that have been shown to trigger negativity.

Julian Treasure is a communications expert and five-time TED Talks speaker. He consults with some of the world's biggest brands on healthier sound environments and trains people to be better listeners. In his work, he has identified several types of communication that increase negativity and make you harder to listen to. The following are most relevant to the interview setting and should be avoided at all costs.

Harsh Judgment

Regardless of how inept your former co-workers were or how bad your previous supervisor was, the interview for your next job is not the place to judge them. If an interviewer asks you about a co-worker or manager that you struggled with, then that is different. In that context, you have been asked to share an experience and the interviewer is anticipating you sharing an experience that will highlight how you overcame negativity. Outside of that context, never bad-mouth previous colleagues. It isn't the memory you want the interviewer to carry with them.

Blaming Others

Interviewers consistently look for candidates who take ownership for their faults because it signals they have the initial ingredient needed to improve. Taking ownership is also important because blaming others is a primary way to be perceived as negative. Blaming is another form of judgment and, whether the facts are true or not, is quickly noticed by interviewers. If you give any answer in which things could have gone better, lean toward taking ownership rather than shifting blame. In the short-term, blame may feel necessary to avoid looking bad. In the long run, it will harm you when the interviewer thinks back on your answers.

Complaining

Listening to someone pass judgment or blame others isn't pleasant. But worse than either of those is listening to someone complain. Complaining combines both harsh judgment and blaming. Even worse, it isn't solution-oriented. If you complain about a previous job, colleague, or supervisor during an interview, you are exhibiting a behavior that every manager loathes. Most managers deal with complaints every day and it isn't a pleasant part of their work. By using the interview to complain, you are triggering negative memories which will impact future reflections of you that you don't want to be associated with.

Make Them Remember a Feeling

Most people stay very professional during interviews. "Professionalism" is most often conveyed as "not emotional." That is a safe choice. But there are times when you want to push the envelope a bit and expressing some emotion is a risk worth taking. An important reason you want to show some emotion is because it shows a level of vulnerability and authenticity that doesn't often happen during interviews and it will make you memorable.

When people think of emotions they would be comfortable exhibiting, they gravitate toward joy and lean away from sadness or anger. All three have the potential to make you stand out in an interview. Joy or happiness about an event is an acceptable emotion to exhibit. Sadness can be shared if you are conveying something that was clearly difficult for you. Anger in the form of acknowledging frustration with an outcome that didn't go your way is also acceptable.

None of these emotions should come through at the same level that you felt them in the moment. In other words, laughing or smiling won't hurt you—but crying might and shouting very certainly will. Instead, the best strategy for sharing emotion is to express in words how you felt during a specific moment. For example, it is perfectly acceptable to say:

- "That experience early in my career made me sad . . ."
- "When I found out about how poorly our team had performed, I was really frustrated that . . ."
- "I had to have tough conversation with a colleague and I really struggled to keep my emotions in check. I still remember that feeling of anger/sadness/shame/fear/ etc."

Verbalizing emotion is not unprofessional. It is human and can be the connection you need with an interviewer who likely has been having dry and emotionless conversations with other candidates.

Any emotion you share will be felt by the interviewer on some level, and that is the secret to why it makes you stand out. When a person we are talking to shares an emotion, we don't just remember the person. We also remember how we felt around that person. We remember how their authenticity ignited our own feelings of being connected as people.

This is an example of an emotional contagion* that works in your favor and the memory it creates drives this strategy. You want people to remember you—and remember themselves.

---

* This concept will be discussed further in the next section.

The interviewer will remember you as someone special because in that moment, they felt something real and different. That ability to stir up a powerful memory, by expressing emotion, gives you a significant edge in the discussion that will happen about you after the interview.

CHANNELING YOUR ANXIETY

Think of a time when you've interacted with someone who was clearly nervous or uncomfortable in some way. Perhaps they were in conversation with you or presenting information to a group. In those moments, when you could tell that the person was anxious, think about yourself. How did you feel?

The answer is very likely that you felt uncomfortable as well. Their discomfort made you anxious. Maybe it was because you felt bad for them, or maybe you just wanted their suffering to end. Whatever the reason, their anxiety negatively impacted you. In psychology, this is called "emotional contagion." The phenomenon has been deeply studied with the common finding that emotions are a form of information that regulate social interactions.[12]

The concept of emotional contagions means that if you control your own emotions, you will also control the interviewer's emotions. You can either make them feel uncomfortable, which isn't the outcome you want, or you can manage your emotions and make them feel comfortable.

If you feel nervous during an interview, the interviewer will know. A little bit of anxiety isn't a bad thing. But in high-pressure situations, like interviews, your anxiety can spiral and leave you in a place that is difficult to recover from. Completely eliminating anxiety isn't the goal. Your nerves exist for a reason. They are a way to mentally and physically prepare you for an interaction. A small amount of nerves is a type of energy that when controlled, can be channeled to your benefit. It is the spiral that you must learn to avoid.

There are many techniques to gain control of anxiety before it impacts the interviewer. The best ones fall within a category called "cognitive reframing," which we'll discuss in the very next chapter. Controlling anxiety is an important skill to have. Learning how to use stress to your benefit is important as well. In this section we will also address both how to mentally shift your energy before entering the interview room and how to turn stress in your favor.

By learning about these techniques and adopting those that best suit your style, you will improve not only your experience, but the interviewer's experience as well. Together, they will continue to shift the odds in your favor.

COGNITIVE REFRAMING

Cognitive reframing is a practice that originated with behavioral therapists who were teaching people how to overcome negative conditions they had created for themselves. Research has shown by reframing the way you perceive a situation, you will change your actual experience in that situation. The practice turns negative events into learning experiences and mistakes into opportunities. Reframing allows people to take a stressor that would otherwise debilitate them and turn it into challenge that strengthens them. Reframing has been shown to not only change your mental or emotional responses, but your physical ones as well.[13]

One of the most powerful and sobering examples of cognitive reframing can be found in a book by Viktor Frankl, *Man's Search for Meaning*. Frankl recounts the three years he spent in several concentration camps during the Second World War. During this time, he suffered starvation, torture, the loss of his entire family, and deaths of fellow inmates. Although Frankl was deeply affected by these occurrences, he constantly reframed the experiences as things to learn from, shape, and turn into material to teach others after his release.

He never let go of that idea. To survive, he turned his mind to lectures he would teach based on what he was witnessing and feeling. His deliberate reframing kept his spirit aloft in the midst of horror. He did survive the camps and used the experience just as he had planned—teaching others to find hope and healing. If Frankl was able to use reframing to overcome his experiences, we can certainly use it to tame the interview.

The following techniques change your thinking patterns and turn interviews from hurdles into stepping stones. They follow an approach that allows you to notice your thoughts, challenge them, and then replace them with thoughts that put you in a winning position.

Say Hello to the Bad Guy

When people experience an emotion, they have increased activity in a region of the brain called the "amygdala." Scientists compare the activation in this part of the brain to hitting the gas when you are driving. If you do nothing, your anxiety will gain momentum, eventually running a red light and ending in disaster. Fortunately, there is another portion of the brain, the right ventrolateral prefrontal cortex, that hits the emotional brakes.

The question is: How do you control that part of the brain and hit the brakes when you are feeling anxious? The answer is: You name it.

A proven technique for controlling anxiety is to literally name it. Researchers conducted a study[14] in which they found that verbalizing an emotion like anxiety, reduces its intensity. When you say the name of the emotion ("nervousness") there is a decrease of the activity associated with that emotion in the amygdala. Naming the emotion causes a counter-increase in the right ventrolateral prefrontal cortex—those are the brakes that slow the feelings down.

What that requires is for you to recognize the initial feeling of anxiety as a yellow light. If you do nothing, you will eventually run a red light. Instead, at that first moment, activate the right ventrolateral prefrontal cortex by saying to yourself, "This is me feeling nervousness. This is just me feeling anxious."

The clinical term for this is "affect labeling" and it has been studied for its ability to manage anxiety, including when it is associated with forms of communication like public speaking.[15] It is effective at controlling emotions because it highlights the gap between reality and feelings. Most importantly, scientists have learned that the specific way you word the phrase is key to making it work.

When you feel anxiety, you start to believe "I am anxious." That becomes a permanent state that only accelerates. To pump the brakes, the words you use must be precise. You cannot say, "I am anxious." Instead you must say, "I am just *feeling* anxious."

That specific wording is a reminder that anxiety is a just feeling, not a self-definition. It puts you back in the driver's seat where you regain control over what the interviewer would have otherwise also felt.

Present-Oriented

Being nervous is an interesting phenomenon. It is associated with feelings such as dread, excitement, apprehension, and fear. Those feelings are correlated with the physical response to stress which is an increase in heart rate and blood pressure and a quickening of the breath, all of which heighten your alertness and energy.* If you weren't in an interview, that physical response wouldn't be a bad one. Your body creates that energy to help you prepare for a threat. Another way to think about this is that anxiety is future-oriented.

Inside the interview room, there is no physical threat approaching. But the body errs on the side of safety and prepares for the future anyway. If left unchecked, the same energy designed to physically engage your body can interfere with your ability to think and communicate clearly. It is that future-orientation which hijacks you during an interview and it is what

---

* We will discuss this concept in more detail, including how to turn it in your favor, in the chapter on breath control.

you must control to improve your performance. The solution is to bring yourself into the present moment.

The reason you get nervous is because you are thinking about the approaching interview. You are feeling the pressure of whether you will do well and what the interviewer will think about you. More specifically, you are thinking about the future outcome. But your present actions determine the future result. Logically then, what happens *after* the interview cannot possibly matter more than what you do *during* the interview.

When you are nervous, you have the order of impact completely reversed. The yet-to-be-written future is controlling the present moment. Because of that reversal of control, you will fall directly into a self-fulfilling prophecy. You will become unnecessarily nervous. You will struggle during the interview and your chance at landing the job will decrease.

To stop this false thinking, you have force yourself to be present-oriented as you enter the interview. Matt Abrahams, a professor of strategic communications at Stanford's Graduate School of Business, has found several techniques that effectively pull you back into the present. These practices help you enter the interview mindful of what needs to be done in the moment. Any or all of them can be done before you enter the location in which you will be interviewed.

Spelling Bee

Look around you at anything that catches your eye and spell it backwards. This serves two purposes. First, it draws you back to your immediate surroundings. Second, the act of translating an image into a word, then into letters, then backwards, forces you to think only about that mental task. You won't think about the future. Take several minutes to do this exercise and you'll find your nervousness beginning to decrease.

The Wrong Thing

Similarly, look at objects around you, but this time make the active effort of calling what you see by the wrong name. If you see a tree, say "horse." When you next look at a bus bench, say "pothole." When you notice a bird, say "orange juice." Continue this for several minutes. You are again forced into the present with a simple activity that removes thoughts of the future and focuses on the now.

Count Backwards

A simpler activity is to start at one hundred and count back to zero—but don't count by ones. Instead count by an unexpected interval, like nine or seventeen. The same present-orientation theory applies. The mind is distracted from a future that is not yet written because it is focusing on a current task that needs a level of concentration that keeps you in the moment. The nervousness is halted and begins to subside.

The goal is not to completely eliminate nervousness. That isn't necessary to succeed during an interview. You just want to control anxiety before it controls you. More importantly, you want to prove to yourself that you can control it. That alone gives you a sense of self-mastery which provides a boost in confidence, which further offsets the nerves. That counterbalance is what you want to feel as you enter the interview.

CONQUERING SELF-DOUBT

Annie Duke is a professional poker player who made history by being the only woman among ten final contestants at the 2004 World Series of Poker. In that world series, she defeated one man after another until she faced the legendary Phil Hellmuth. In a showdown of skill, mental prowess, and strategy, Duke eventually beat Hellmuth to take home the $2 million prize.

By the time Annie Duke was sitting at that table facing Hellmuth, she had been playing—and winning—poker for ten years. Yet she recalls the intense self-doubt she felt during the entire tournament. She wondered if she truly deserved to be at the table with her male counterparts and whether EPSN had only invited her because of the "good optics" that having a woman presented. There is no question she deserved to be there. But her concern that she would be judged for her gender rather than her skill had the real potential of impacting her performance.

Fortunately, Annie was a highly successful poker player who was often the only woman at the poker table. That experience had taught her how control her self-doubt and how to use negative perceptions others had of her to give her strength. The self-doubt she felt and its ability to affect her performance has been extensively researched and has a unique name— "stereotype threat."

Stereotype Threat
Claude Steele and Joshua Aronson are social scientists, one from Stanford University and the other from the University of Texas at Austin. They conducted a groundbreaking study on

the effect of self-doubt. Their study was on the effect of negative stereotypes about one's own group and how it could become a self-fulfilling prophecy. Through their research, Steel and Aronson gained a deeper understanding of this phenomenon.

In their study, they gathered data on the performance of Black and White students on academic tests. Black students unfortunately face a persistent stereotype that they are not as intelligent as White students. The researchers wanted to understand the impact of this stereotype on how the Black students perceived *themselves* and by extension, how this impacted their behavior.

Steele and Aronson discovered that when the test instructors emphasized the role of race before the test, then Black students did not perform as well as White students. But when race was not mentioned, the students did equally well across racial lines. Steele and Aronson labeled this "stereotype threat," indicating that when anyone experiences self-doubt due to a negative belief about themselves, they perform worse.

This phenomenon has been replicated hundreds of times and doesn't only affect Black students. When White students were told that a physical performance was an indicator of their physical abilities, they performed worse. While Black students are often stereotyped as intellectually less competent, White students are often stereotyped as physically less competent. Both are stereotypes, but when White students were reminded of their stereotype, they performed worse. Similarly, when women were asked to take a math test but were first told that women usually don't do well in math, they performed worse than their male counterparts.

Your Full Potential
Self-doubt has a powerful impact on our ability to live up to our full potential. What begins in the mind easily turns into

behaviors that are self-defeating. The impact, however, goes even deeper than behavior. All of us have a cognitive function called "working memory," which allows us to simultaneously track multiple strands of information and stay focused. Working memory is diminished when we go into a state of heightened stress. The stress brought on by self-doubt diverts energy away from working memory and toward managing other emotions. Not only does self-doubt make us behave differently, our ability to handle information also decreases.

Fortunately, research on stereotype threat has shown there are ways to conquer self-doubt. Because self-doubt takes hold in the mind first, it must be attacked in the mind first. Two practices—"powerful thinking" and "value-affirmation"—are versions of a therapeutic approach called "expressive writing" that will help you manage self-doubt. The approach is well-researched and impacts many areas of mental functioning including your working memory,[16] where the positive effect sometimes lasts for weeks afterward.

During an interview you want to live up to your full potential. Interviewing is a test of performance, and just like any other test of performance, it will be impacted by unchecked self-doubt. But when we turn to the science, the following techniques have shown that you can absolutely train your mind to resist intrusive and destructive thoughts.

Not Positive Thinking, Powerful Thinking

Research has found that the act of self-affirmation can negate the impact of self-doubt.[17] This goes beyond just thinking positive thoughts. While positive thinking is valuable, in moments of higher-than-normal stress, you need to write down specific powerful thoughts about your strengths. These don't have to be the strengths needed for the job. They are your strengths, in general. For example:

- I am a great soccer player.
- I spend a lot of time with my kids and am a great parent.
- I've travelled to twenty states and can talk with anyone about US geography.

Once you've listed them, reflect on the underlying strength that allows the attribute to rise to the top.

- I'm great at soccer because I've got strong instincts.
- I'm a great parent because I value people and helping others.
- Traveling a lot has made me grateful and appreciative of the little things.

Do this writing exercise the evening before an interview. Keep the list of strengths with you and before you enter the building for your interview, repeat the list out loud to yourself. While the idea of self-affirmation has become cliché, this is more than self-affirmation. This practice self-affirms and then provides specific evidence. Even when these powerful thoughts aren't related to the job you are interviewing for, they serve as a reminder of how strong you are, period. And that will have a positive impact on your performance.

Value-Affirmation

A similar exercise can be done with a reflection on your values.[18] We are driven by our values. They are core to us and a source of strength. They are what defines us and can't be taken from us. Reflecting on your values shortly before an interview provides self-affirmation of who you are. But more importantly, it removes the focus on what others may think you are. When this tactic was used by college students, they found it made them less susceptive to self-doubt and its negative impact on performance.

For this technique, write down several of your values and again, add specifics:

- I value honesty because . . .
- I value friendship because . . .
- I value hard work because . . .

The evening before an interview, do this exercise to capture who you are. Then review what you've written shortly before the interview. The research found that writing about your values and illustrating why they matter reduces the concern about how others will judge you. Concern about what others think of you is common when interviewing, but it is the seed of self-doubt. Plant a different seed. Plant seeds about your values and that truth will take hold and push away self-doubt.

The Learning Reframe
The interview is a setting in which you are clearly being judged to determine whether you are worthy of working for the organization that is assessing you. It is the perfect environment for making even the most confident person feel self-doubt. For those of us who are not confident to begin with, the self-doubt can be crippling.

If that feels as though it applies to you, simply reframing your self-doubts may not be effective enough. In those cases, a better way to reframe self-doubt is to completely reframe the upcoming experience[19] itself. This tactic allows you to mentally reframe the purpose of the interview. Most people perceive interviews as a test of their ability. People who successfully reframe interviews don't see them that way. They turn it 180 degrees. Rather than perceiving it as a test, they see interviews as a learning experience. They tell themselves they are going into the experience to learn about the interviewer, the job, the organization and, most importantly, about themselves.

They reframe the questions they will be asked as opportunities to better understand themselves. They also view the interview as an opportunity to learn how to become better communicators. This repositioning lowers their anxiety and self-doubt because it makes the interview less about their performance and more about what they can learn from the experience. This increases their confidence because one way or another, the experience of interviewing will end well for them.

Use Self-Doubt to Your Advantage

Earlier in this section we discussed "affect labeling" and how you can control an emotion by naming it. Self-doubt can be controlled in a similar way. Research has shown that teaching people about self-doubt or stereotype threat lessens its impact. So, if you become anxious before an interview, remind yourself that it's due to self-doubt, not due to an actual failure that you will commit. Labeling it gives you more control over it.

By recognizing self-doubt when it shows up, you can harness it to propel you. Research calls this the "reappraisal of arousal."[20] Researchers have found that when you notice an energy like self-doubt, you are doing more than just recognizing it as a barrier to performance. Self-doubt, when recognized, transforms from an energy that works against you to an energy that improves performance.

The good news is that the same way your mind can create hurdles, whether for good reason or not, your mind can find ways to overcome those hurdles. If you are a person who has lower self-confidence or often finds yourself doubting your own abilities, then begin doing research on self-doubt and stereotype threat. By educating yourself about these phenomena, you'll recognize them when they arrive. Knowledge of how they work will not only demystify them but allow you to harness and redirect them. Where self-doubt once held you back, its recognition will begin to propel you forward.

BREATH CONTROL

So far, we discussed practices for managing your anxiety or stress by managing your mind. Now let's turn to channeling nervous energy, but this time, by using your body.

For nearly two hundred thousand years, the human mind has managed what award-winning professor Mark Leary calls an "immediate-return environment."[21] For most of our existence, humans have lived in environments where our actions deliver an immediate outcome. Physical survival was the main driver of our actions. Whether this meant avoiding danger, finding food, or searching for shelter.

In that paradigm, anxiety and stress were helpful because they helped humans solve immediate and potentially life-threatening problems. Anxiety increases your heart rate and sends more blood to your brain, improving its ability to assess, decipher, and react. One of the primary theories about anxiety, stress, and other emotions is they exist to organize all our cognitive functions at any given moment. In today's world you may experience anxiety as a negative experience. But in the past, it quickened your thinking and sharpened your senses. This is what scientists refer to as the "organizing power of anxiety."[22]

That organizing power can be a powerful benefit to you. But psychologists have shown that in our present-day environments, we often misinterpret[23] the instinctual signals our mind is sending. During an interview the immediate perceived threat is the interview itself. Even if only slightly, your heart will beat more quickly and your blood pressure will elevate. Since we are removed from the physical conditions of the past in which we instinctually knew what to do with this change, anxiety and stress weigh on us rather than elevate us. They impair our cognitive skills and makes us stumble rather than soar.

This occurs because during an interview, anxiety is mistakenly telling you to run. But, during an interview, you need to organize your senses, stand your ground, and fight for what is yours—the job. To prepare for that fight, you must use the mechanism your body has that can organize the energy which comes from increased blood flow, anxiety, and stress—your breathing.

Diaphragmatic Breathing
According to the University of Michigan Medical School,[24] breathing is how you physically send messages to your brain to redirect it. Researchers at the university found that deep breathing techniques are very effective ways to manage stress in your body. The important distinction is that you aren't trying to eliminate stress. You want to manage it, because a certain level of it will sharpen your thinking.

The best way to manage our anxiety is to use diaphragmatic breathing, also known as belly breathing, deep breathing, or paced respiration. The University of Michigan isn't alone in promoting this practice. The majority of medical schools recommend diaphragmatic breathing, including Harvard University, which has published breathing practices for turning anxiety into a positive tool. In their words: "When appropriately invoked, the stress response helps us rise to many challenges."[25]

Diaphragmatic breathing is the way our bodies were designed to breathe. Modern society, however, has made it seem unnatural to us. Research from Harvard suggests this misperception stems from lifestyles in which we sit too much, coupled with beauty standards that suggest keeping our stomach sucked in is better than using it to help us breathe. Whatever the reason, managing your breath gives you a competitive edge in moments like interviewing. You don't need to enroll in yoga or tai chi to take control of your breath. Several self-facilitated deep-breathing techniques, recommended by experts across the spectrum, can be done with a little independent practice. Just as importantly, they can be done while seated and therefore should be done before you leave your car to enter the interview.

Belly Breathing

This is the simplest and easiest exercise to do. Whether you feel anxious or not, take three minutes before your interview to take control with the following steps:

- Sit upright in a comfortable position.
- Place one hand on your stomach just below your ribs. Place your other hand on your chest.
- Inhale slowly through your nose. Think about the air going into your stomach first and let your belly push your hand out. Your chest should not move.
- Exhale through pursed lips, almost as if whistling. The hand on your belly should go in. Continue to draw your stomach in to push all the air out.
- Repeat this breath eight to ten times. Don't rush.

4-7-8 Breathing

This is the same as belly breathing but it gives you specific timing to follow. Once you've gotten a feel for what belly breathing feels like, this can be used to increase your sense of control. One of the issues with belly breathing is you won't know if you are going too fast or too slow. 4-7-8 breathing gives you timing to follow and a sense of security knowing you are doing it correctly.

- Sit upright in a comfortable position.
- Place one hand on your stomach just below your ribs. Place your other hand on your chest.
- Inhale slowly through your nose. Think about the air going into your stomach first and let your belly push your hand out. Your chest should not move. *Silently count to four as you breathe in.*
- *Hold your breath and silently count to seven.*
- Exhale through pursed lips, almost as if whistling. The hand on your belly should go in. *As you are breathing out, silently count to eight. Try to time it such that when you reach eight, you've exhaled all the air.*
- Repeat this breath five to eight times. Don't rush.

Roll Breathing

Roll breathing simply takes belly breathing up one notch by helping you completely use your lungs from bottom to top, literally. It focuses on the rhythm of your breath which also helps with focus and preparation.

- Begin by doing the belly breathing exercise above five times. You are doing this just to get the initial motion correct.
- After five deep belly breaths in—during which only the belly expands, and the chest remains still—take the next breath the same way, by inhaling into your lower lungs, but then continue inhaling into your upper chest.
- The rhythm will be such that your belly expands first, then your chest, and as your chest expands you will feel your stomach go in a little bit.

- Now when you exhale—again, almost as if whistling—your stomach should empty first (feel it with your hand), then your chest should empty last.
- This will create a rolling motion. Continue this for three to five minutes.

Although Western medical schools have recently adopted these breathing techniques, they have been promoted for thousands of years in Eastern medicine practices. They have long been proven to be simple ways to control the complexities of fight or flight. They will give you the balance needed to increase your focus and attention and heighten your performance. As legendary tai chi master Lee Holden is often quoted saying, "We have to breathe anyway. We might as well be breathing efficiently and with power."

LAUGHTER

There is a growing body of research about the impact of humor on relationships and communication. Some researchers work to understand how humor originates in the mind of the person being humorous, while others search to learn how humor impacts those on the receiving end. For example, people who are humorous are viewed more positively by others, and more likely to be perceived as popular. Without a doubt, humor is seen as a positive mechanism for communicating.

The effectiveness of humor in communications is entirely driven by context. Context includes not only the setting, but the past experience of the listener, culture, unspoken norms, and a host of other factors you may not be aware of. For this reason, using humor during an interview is risky.

But that doesn't mean humor can't be utilized to your advantage. While you need to be cautious about using humor during an interview, using humor as a way to prepare for an interview and improve your performance is scientifically proven and highly recommended. Multiple studies[26] have found that enjoying something humorous changes your brain wave activity. Laughter increases endorphins which send dopamine to your brain and shifts your brain toward a "gamma frequency." This change lowers your blood pressure and reduces the hormones that cause stress. Just as relevant for interviews, the research has shown this same effect also improves your ability to recall memories.

To improve your interview performance, use laughter strategically. At some point before the interview, either while you are still at home or during the drive to the interview, listen to a humorous podcast, YouTube clip, or medium of your choice.

Your instinct may tell you that you should do something more serious with that time. Perhaps you should be rehearsing examples of answers you will give or reviewing your resume. But the days leading up to the interview are the best time to do that. The moments immediately before the interview are about getting in the right state of mind. They are about becoming the person you want to be when you enter the room.

Like the many athletes we've all seen who have a routine or ritual they execute before hitting the field, you too need to find what works for you. Your performance won't be as physically demanding, but the mental and emotional aspect of successfully interviewing require the same approach. Whether it's becoming present-oriented, laughing, breathing correctly, or a mix of them all, don't underestimate the value of mental preparation just before game time.

SECTION FOUR

How to use time, sleep, and practice to boost your interview performance.

POWER #9

CONTROLLING TIME

Whenever the history of persuasion is discussed, ethos, pathos, and logos are the three most commonly mentioned elements. But scholars in the field will point out a fourth element that is often overlooked. That element is "kairos." Many people are not familiar with it, and those who have heard of it often confuse it with a similar word—"chronos."

Both words represent the concept of time and have their origins in Greek mythology. Chronos, however, is embedded in our language with words like "chronology," "synchronicity," and "chronometer." As a result, when we think of time, we think of the word "chronos." But chronos and kairos are very different. Chronos represents the measurement of time. If chronos were framed as a question, it would be, "How long?" Chronos is about the passing of time.

Kairos, on the other hand, is about a moment in time. If kairos were framed as a question, it would be, "When?" Kairos is a practice that has been applied in a range of fields from rhetoric to religion to science. Depending on the field of study, it can represent the strategy of finding the right time, or it can mean strategically creating an opening or opportunity. In ancient Greece, the entrance to the Olympia Stadium had two

167

statues on either side. One was Hermes, the god of luck. The other was Kairos, the god of the moment. A poem written in the third century was inscribed under his statue and captures the essence of what the concept means:

Who are you?
Kairos, who conquered everything.
Why do you tiptoe?
I run quickly.
Why do you have wings on your feet?
I fly like the wind.
Why do you carry a razor in your hand?
To remind people that I'm sharper than a knife.
Why does a lock of hair fall on your forehead?
So that I can be seized by whoever meets me.
Why are you bald on the back of your head?
Once my winged feet pass by, even if desiring to, no one will catch me from behind.
For what reason did the artist fashion you?
For your sake, stranger, and he placed me at the entrance as a lesson.

Kairos is about timing. It represents a strategy in which you use time to your advantage. This section is about that definition of time. We'll first focus on punctuality. That topic may seem like "Interview Basics 101," but think about the last time you were late to something. Did you plan to be late? Of course not, no one intends to be late. But research shows that is precisely why people are late. The science behind never being late is invaluable for a candidate.

Next, we'll discuss the best time of day to interview. Getting hired is important. But, to give perspective on its level of importance, we'll look at daily decisions made in hospitals and the legal system. In those arenas, decisions determine whether someone lives, dies, or loses their freedom. Research in those fields indicates that the accuracy of decisions is linked to the time of day they are made. Those same discoveries apply to interviewers and candidates.

Finally, we'll share a sophisticated strategy that allows you to strengthen any answer you provide by adjusting the *tense* in which you answer. It turns out that answering a question in the past, present, or future tense can change how that answer is perceived.

WHY CLOTHES AND COFFEE MAKE YOU LATE

In a survey[1] of hiring managers, 93 percent stated being late hurts a candidate's chances more than anything else. Lack of punctuality was ranked worse than being underqualified, answering questions incorrectly, rambling, lack of preparation, and multiple other factors that should matter more. If you believe focusing on punctuality is an outdated way of thinking or that this research is skewed by workstyles of older managers—you're making a mistake. The 93 percent who viewed being late as negative, were young managers themselves. The percentage that viewed late candidates poorly only went up from there and reached 99 percent for managers in their fifties.

Here is what's interesting. Science has shown that being late may not be as bad as it seems. A study conducted by psychologists at San Diego State University and Penn State University found that people who are consistently late are better at stress-management and multitasking.[2] Research by Diana Delonzor, Fortune 500 consultant and author of *Never Be Late Again*, found that people who are late tend to be more optimistic. This optimism translates to more positive beliefs about what they can accomplish and the valuable "can-do attitude" that employers want.

Unfortunately, these new findings are not going to help you. The reality is most people aren't aware of this new research. In addition, research shows the *perception* of unpunctuality as a negative trait is so engrained in our psyche that even when faced with new information, it continues to prevail.[3] Despite new research, despite every legitimate reason you might have for being late, despite only being a few minutes late—if you are late to an interview it is automatically a strike against you.

The strategy to fix this might seem simple. Just don't be late.

But science tells us the apparent simplicity of being on time is exactly why people end up being late. Psychologists Daniel Kahneman and Amos Tversky named this phenomenon "the planning fallacy." The planning fallacy suggests that people underestimate their ability to be punctual by failing to accurately predict how long tasks will take. The amount they underestimate isn't minor. Research has shown the average miscalculation is 40 percent.[4]

According to this research, the same positive traits mentioned previously—optimism and the ability to multitask—might be valuable once hired, but as a candidate they are disastrous.

The researchers discovered that we are often late because we tend to be more optimistic about our ability to be on time. If you couple optimism with multitasking, things get even worse on an interview day. Science tells us if you believe you multitask well under pressure, the type you might find on an interview day, odds are *higher* that you actually won't multitask well.[5]

To overcome this dilemma, you have to go into the interview day assuming you will be late. Don't allow optimism to cloud your thinking. Go the other direction. *Be pessimistic and remove as many of the other tasks you will need to do that day.* There are two specific areas in how you normally operate that you need to rethink and adjust—clothes and coffee.

Clothes

We've discussed the importance of thinking about what to wear. Now let's talk about the importance of *when* you should decide what to wear.

Getting dressed not only takes a considerable amount of time, it is time that you will underestimate. Solve this problem by choosing and trying on what you will wear *two days* before the interview. This practice removes anything unexpected from delaying the day of your interview. Think back on the number of times you've tried on an outfit and suddenly realized there was a stain you forgot about, or a button missing, or it simply didn't make you look or feel the way you mentally envisioned. This consistently happens when people get dressed the day of the interview.

Be pessimistic. Assume all those things will happen and get dressed two days before the interview. That will give you time to take an item to the cleaners, or spot clean, or work through multiple outfits to find just the right one. Once you've found what you will wear, put it aside until the interview day and you've just removed a significant source of stress and a primary barrier to arriving on time.

Coffee

Some people can't function unless they have a cup of coffee. Caffeine is a stimulant that affects your central nervous system, increasing your energy and alertness. These are good things. Stopping and grabbing a cup a coffee on our way to anything—including an interview—has become embedded into our daily routines. It is embedded in our work culture and feels completely normal. And that is where the problem arises.

A common gripe among interviewers is about the candidate who arrives late to an interview, with a steaming cup of fresh coffee in their hand. People lose time on interview days by sticking to their normal routine. While caffeine can improve your performance, it can cause you to run behind because you assume your quick stop to grab a cup of coffee will run as smoothly as it usually does. The addiction won't let you skip the coffee because you need it to function that morning.

Pessimism is crucial again. You need to assume that on the day of your interview, the line inside the coffee shop (as well as the drive-through) will be longer than usual. Assume your normal routine will make you late. Instead, buy cold coffee the night before. Or if you need hot coffee, buy it the night before and pop it in the microwave that morning. That won't be as delicious as a new cup. But on the day of an interview, flavor isn't the goal. The goal is adjusting your routine, so you still get the caffeine hit without the addiction causing you to be late.

THE RETURN TRIP EFFECT

Now that you've removed clothes and coffee, you need an insurance policy. That policy comes in the form of understanding a phenomenon called "the return trip effect."

Have you ever driven somewhere for the first time and then when you drive back from the same place, it seems faster? This phenomenon has puzzled researchers for years because the distance between the two locations is the same, but the passage of time is perceived differently. Researchers have named this mental flaw "the return trip effect."

An initial explanation for the effect was the trip back is more familiar and therefore time seems to move faster. In other words, during the first trip your brain spends more energy processing new inputs and therefore the duration seems longer. More recently, researchers[6] at Tilburg University in the Netherlands uncovered another explanation. These researchers realized it was less about familiarity and more about what they termed a "violation of expectations."

It turns out people aren't only bad at determining how long *a task* will take, as Kahneman and Tversky discovered, they are also bad at estimating how long it takes *to get somewhere*. In the Tilburg studies, participants felt the return trip was 22 percent shorter than the first trip.

Add a Third

You now have two important pieces of science to help you never be late. Kahneman and Tvserky found we miscalculate the length of tasks by 40 percent. The researchers at Tilburg University found we misjudge the amount of time it takes to travel somewhere by 22 percent.

If you've never been to the place where you are interviewing, use the center of that range (22–40 percent), and assume it will take roughly a third longer than you think to get there. If you think it will take thirty minutes, give yourself forty minutes. If you think it will take an hour, budget an hour and twenty minutes.

The immediate reaction might be to simply plug the distance into your GPS system (Waze, Google Maps, etc.) and get an accurate estimation. But that only tells you how long it takes to get to the building. Not how long it takes to get to the location of the interview in the building. That is again where people dramatically underestimate and end up being late.

To make this very clear, imagine mapping the distance to an interview. You mentally give yourself an additional ten minutes to park and take the elevator up to the interview. Then, when you arrive at the interview you learn that the parking lot is on one side of a huge office complex and your interview is on the opposite side. And you still need to get through security. The ten minutes you allotted is now eaten up by you speed-walking through the complex, checking into security, waiting for the elevator, and making a pit-stop at the restroom to dab at the sweat pouring from your face.

Avoid all of this by mapping how long it will take to drive to the interview. Then mentally add whatever additional time you think you might need (parking, security, elevator, etc.).

When you've done all that, add another third.

For Those Who Don't Like to Be Early

Researcher Adoree Durayappah[7] found another interesting reason why some people are late—they don't like to be early. Some people view being early as inefficient. To them, it is a waste of their time to sit and wait. They also feel it intrudes on the time of the person who now knows you are waiting for them.

If you fall into this category, you have to understand that even if your beliefs are accurate, during an interview day, the rules are different. While there are still some interviewers who are annoyed by candidates who arrive early, they are heavily outnumbered by those who favorably view people who are early. In a survey[8] of nearly 850 hiring managers, 75 percent viewed arriving early as a positive trait.

If 75 percent of interviewers view a behavior as positive, then play those odds. Take all the necessary steps so you won't be late, then build in even more time—and get there early.

THE BEST TIME TO INTERVIEW

The work of doctors, nurses, lawyers, and judges directly determines life outcomes. Therefore, learning how they can make better decisions has been the focus of a considerable amount of research. That research has led to many discoveries about how changes in the behavior of practitioners can save lives. While interviewers are not making life or death decisions, the underlying cognitive factors that impact quality of thinking apply to them as well. An important and relevant body of research to apply to the interview setting is about how the *time of day* affects decision-making.

Occasionally, a sobering story will make the headlines about a patient who entered the hospital for a routine procedure but ended up dying due to an anesthesia-related error. This is more common than one would hope. Because of this, studies have been conducted to understand why.

A significant driver of these errors is the time of day that the anesthesia is given. The Duke University Hospital conducted a study in which they reviewed approximately 90 thousand surgeries to identify mistakes made or harm caused due to anesthesiologists. What they discovered was eye-opening. The odds of a mistake happening at 9 a.m. was about 1 percent. The odds of a mistake happening after 3 p.m. was four times higher at slightly above 4 percent.[9]

A similar phenomenon can be found in the judicial system where a defendant's freedom or imprisonment hinges on a judge's evidence-based decision. That statement, it turns out, isn't quite accurate. Multiple studies have found that verdicts don't only hinge on evidence presented to the judge, but the time of day that the judge makes the decision.[10]

For example, research examining decisions made by parole boards found that judges were more likely to make decisions in favor of the criminal in the morning but by the afternoon, favorable decisions dropped significantly. The study controlled for multiple factors including the offense itself and characteristics of the offender. The impact of the timing of the decisions continued to hold true. In the afternoon, judges gave harsher sentences.

The effect of timing on decision-making is so powerful that an entire book has been written on the topic. Daniel Pink's book, *When*, makes it clear the effect reaches beyond anesthesiologists and judges. Pink cites study after study demonstrating the same effect in the administration of antibiotics, colonoscopies, hand hygiene in hospitals, vehicular accidents, ethical behavior, and academic performance on tests. In all these instances, decision-making and cognitive performance both declined in the afternoon.

In his book, Pink shows how the overlap between time of day and decision-making also extends into the business world. A survey[11] conducted in Britain and published in *Medical Daily* pinpointed the exact time of day found to be least productive for employees. It isn't surprising that their research indicated that time to also be in the afternoon—at 2:55 p.m.

It doesn't take much to see how the time of day that an interview occurs can either help or hurt a candidate. The takeaway for candidates is simple—if you can choose what time to have your interview, choose the morning. Stay away from interviews in the afternoon.

Interviewers, like judges, make complex decisions based on many inputs. In the courtroom, if the judge assumes innocence and is wrong, more people will be exposed to a criminal they've freed. If they assume guilt and are wrong, they only harm one person's life. Those trade-offs and risks aren't minor, and judges weigh them heavily. But in the afternoon, judges have less cognitive power. In those moments, the safer and simpler decision for judges is to assume guilt.

For interviewers, the path they choose in the interview isn't about guilt, but it is about risk. In the afternoon, the interviewer's brain is more likely to choose the simpler path of assuming the candidate in front of them isn't worth the risk of potentially not being a strong employee. As a result, the decision is more likely to be "no."

To maximize the odds of the interviewer saying "yes" to your candidacy, choose an interview slot that begins at 10:30 a.m.* or earlier. You may be tempted to take an 11 a.m. interview. That might be safe, but if you have a choice, avoid those as well. Some of the same research on time of day has shown a decrease in effective decision-making shortly before lunch when decision-makers are hungry. Given that lunch is typically around 12 p.m. or 1 p.m., the 11 a.m. interview slot can have increased risk.

Research also shows that decision-making does improve shortly after lunch (or any break that restores energy). But since it is hard to predict when your interviewer had lunch (or took their last break), the best way to manage the odds is to try to get a morning interview slot.

If you are given an afternoon slot, politely ask if there are any opportunities that same week in the morning. This isn't an odd question to ask. If you are currently employed, you can say that stepping away from your current job is difficult to manage in the afternoon. If you are out of work, use any predetermined obligation as a reason for the requested switch. e.g., picking up children from school, picking up a parent from an

---

* The same survey that found 2:55 p.m. to be least productive for employees also found 10:26 a.m. to be the most productive.

airport, a doctor's appointment, etc. The worst that can happen is that they can't accommodate you. If that happens, don't despair. The time of the interview is only one of many ways to control the interview and you'll find many other ways to shift the odds toward you.

You won't always be able to control when your interview will happen. But by not attempting to control the time, you are giving up power. Don't commit this unforced error. Always ask for a 10:30 a.m. interview slot or earlier.*

---

* Some studies have shown Mondays and Fridays are not optimal for interviewing. But controlling for the perfect day and time is not a strong strategy. Try to get a good interview time but spend far more energy on what you do during that time.

HOW TO USE THE PAST, PRESENT, AND FUTURE TENSE

At first glance the following strategy will seem simple. In short, if you change the "tense" in which you respond to a question, you change what the listener thinks about the answer. That doesn't sound complicated, but it is worth noting that in execution, you may find it too complex to layer into the many other things you'll be balancing during an interview. It is worth understanding, however, so you can determine if it is something you want to invest in using.

Let's begin by explaining what we mean by the word "tense." Quite often when interviewers ask questions, they are referencing the past. For example:

> Interviewer: *Can you give me an example of a time when you managed a project with a limited budget?*

According to researchers, there are two problems with trying to make a point using the past. First, the past is associated with blame. Second, the past can't be changed.* Whatever answer you provide has a sense of finality to it. It defines you. So, if your answer provides an example that ends well, then that works in your favor. But sometimes the only example you can share is one with an average outcome. In that scenario, the blame rests on you and defines you.

Fortunately, you have two other tenses in your toolbox to strengthen any answer you give—the present and future tense.

---

* Aristotle called this the "judicial argument" and it is often used in courtrooms.

When you are preparing examples to share, make sure to prepare some examples that are happening in the present and, if possible, in the future.

Let's begin with the present tense to see how that works. When an interviewer asks you a question about the past:

Interviewer: *Can you give me an example of a time when you managed a project with a limited budget?*

If relevant, you have the control to provide an answer in the present tense.

Candidate: *Yes, I'm actually working on a project like that now . . .*

The benefit of answering in the present tense shifts the answer from the past (where blame and finality can be attributed) to the present, which researchers have found is more likely to inspire and put the listener in an ideal state of mind.*

Using the present to answer a question has a few downsides. First, if you don't have a current project with which to answer this question, then you can't use it. Second, it relies heavily on what persuasion experts called the "demonstrative technique." In other words, you need to be a good storyteller to share an answer which may end with, "The project isn't finished yet, so we'll see what the outcomes are soon."

For this reason, most experts favor incorporating the future tense. The future is malleable. The future is a place where you can verbally take the interviewer and tell them what they will

---

* This type of language is found less in courtrooms and more in the speeches of great orators.

see. If you are telling what will happen in the future, the listener may have doubts, but it is harder for them to paint a different picture. In the past and present there is still room for "right" and "wrong." Using the future tense is called the "deliberative" argument. It rests on choices you say you will make and the interviewer, without realizing it, accepting your version of the future.

This does not mean you are going to give examples from the future. What it does mean is that any time an interviewer asks a question, you should answer it honestly in the past or present tense:

- "I once had a project like that, and I . . ."
- "I am currently working on a project like that, and I am . . ."

But you must *always* end your answer in the future tense:

- "I once had a project like that, and I . . . (describe your project) . . . And as I look forward, because of that project I now know how to do X and Y next time around."

Or

- "I once had a project like that, and I . . . (describe your project) . . . And as I look forward, because of that project, next time I will be much stronger at Z."

This structure allows you to give an example, that may have been mediocre—either because of how you told it or because the results were average. But it still ends in the future where you are better.

Similarly, you should use the same structure with a present tense answer:

- "I am currently working a project like that, and I am . . . (describe your project) . . . The project isn't finished yet, but there are a few things I am certain about. We will accomplish X and Y. In addition, my ability to do Z will be even stronger because of this project."

If you give an example in the present tense, *never* end it with an answer that concludes with:

- ". . . and we are still in the middle of the project so we don't know how it will end."

That allows the interviewer to decide what your future looks like. Their decision will depend on what they've heard from you so far, your delivery of the answer, or any other signals they've received. Don't leave that in their control. They may already have an opinion, positive or otherwise. Continue to influence it by telling them what the future will be.

Whether they fully believe it or not isn't the point. The fact that you've introduced the future you want as a possibility, shifts odds toward you.

THE TRUTH ABOUT SLEEP

R esearch on the relationship between sleep and peak performance has consistently shown a direct correlation between the two. While we often think of sleep in relation to physical performance, its connection to mental performance is just as significant.

A lack of sleep increases risk of injury and weight gain while decreasing muscle recovery, glycogen production, and general motor function. For mental performance, insufficient sleep negatively impacts motivation, focus, stress regulation, judgment, situational awareness, memory, and learning. The research not only supports the importance of sufficient sleep, it also provides sleep techniques that can strategically be used to improve performance.

Similar to athletic performance, to win the interview you need to be operating at your best. A deficit in any of the mental factors mentioned will impact how well you interview.* There

---

* If the argument that sleep supports peak performance isn't convincing, then it is worth noting studies show inadequate sleep impairs the brain the same way alcohol does. If you don't feel the need to deliver a performance worthy of an elite athlete, you should consider whether you'd go to an interview even slightly intoxicated.

are two interview strategies that involve sleep. First, due to a mix of misinformation and anecdotal personal experiences, we consistently underestimate or overestimate how much sleep we need. Second, the ability to use sleep as a preparation technique has been widely proven, but rarely applied to the context of interviews. In this section, we'll tackle both.

HOW MANY HOURS OF SLEEP MAXIMIZE PERFORMANCE?

L et's begin with the answer. Despite everything we continue to hear about getting *eight* hours of sleep, this number is wrong. A multitude of studies has shown the amount needed for optimal performance is—*seven* hours. Research has also addressed the fact that we all differ slightly in our specific needs, and therefore a slightly wider range is recommended as the guideline—6.5 to 7.5 hours.

Anything less will decrease your cognitive functioning. Interestingly, so will anything more.

When it comes to our beliefs about how much sleep we individually need to function well, we are led astray by several common narratives. The first consists of the stories about people who only need four to five hours of sleep to function well. These people are held up as heroes and revered for their abilities. We want to be that type of person. In our culture, particularly corporate culture, the ability to operate on little sleep has become a badge of honor. Second is the idea that even if we aren't like the legends who need little sleep, losing an hour of sleep won't dramatically impact us the following day. Third is the often-cited data point that we need eight hours of sleep to function properly.

All these narratives are misleading. Believing in them will set you up for failure. Let's quickly dispel each of them to reset our understanding of how much sleep you truly need to operate at your best.

According to HelpGuide, an organization focused on mental health, only 3 percent of the population has the genetic trait that allows them to sleep six hours or less and still perform optimally. It is in your best interest to assume you are in the 97 percent who needs more than six hours. They also provide clarity on the second piece of misinformation. Their studies show that while losing just one hour of sleep may not cause you to nod off during the day, it does affect your capacity to think effectively and respond quickly.

The misunderstanding continues to live on because the accurate information runs counter to the anecdotal experiences we've all had when we've slept too little in the past. In those instances, unless we lost several hours of sleep, we still felt attentive and focused the following day. Because of this, we've told ourselves that losing a little sleep can't be such a bad thing. But research has shown that while people with too little sleep don't have a problem focusing on a specific issue, they do have a problem staying focused over an extended set of issues—like those faced during an interview.

We all lose focus sometimes, that's natural. If you've had enough sleep, you realize it and can refocus. But if you haven't had enough sleep, you don't realize that you've lost focus. Instead you proceed through the interview believing you are focused. You will exit the interview feeling as though you've done well, although there were multiple instances of subpar answers and lost opportunities to improve them.

Numerous studies have debunked the various myths and misunderstandings that are part of the "eight hours of sleep" narrative. A study[12] conducted by researchers at the University of California, San Francisco found the optimal number to be seven hours of sleep. Psychologist Shawn Youngstedt reported the same results in an interview with the *Wall Street Journal*.[13] Daniel Kripke, one of the most acclaimed researchers on sleep and co-director of research at the Scripps Clinic Sleep Center, prefers to provide[14] the range of 6.5 to 7.5 hours of sleep.

The range is important to keep in mind because studies have shown that sleeping *more* than eight hours has a *negative* impact on mental functioning and can be just as bad as sleeping too little. In one study, researchers found cognitive performance peaked at seven hours, worsening with more rest.[15] Another study involving 5,177 participants in their thirties from a cross-section of the population, found the same results led to decreased verbal fluency and lower retention of verbal material.

These findings are directly connected to interview performance and the takeaway is not complicated. Stay in the 6.5 to 7.5 hours of sleep range. If you are getting less than 6.5 hours or more than 7.5 hours, you are committing an unforced error that research shows could be as bad as getting nearly no sleep at all.[16]

THE LINK BETWEEN SLEEP AND PRACTICE

The importance of sleep goes beyond optimal performance during the interview. When used strategically, it can also be used to maximize your preparation in the days leading up to the interview.

For any interview, you will have to do some type of preparation. That preparation will include reviewing answers to potential questions, researching the organization and role, gathering information about the industry, and learning about the people who will be interviewing you, among other things.

The secret to maximizing this preparation is to do it in the evenings shortly before you go to sleep. Studies suggest that sleeping shortly after we learn new information improves our ability to retain and then recall that information later. A reason this may occur is because one of the functions of the hippocampus, a region of our brain, is like a computer's cache memory. As we sleep, the hippocampus sends information it has gathered to the neocortex, which serves as long-term storage and where it can be accessed in the future.

Matthew Walker—professor of neuroscience and psychology at the UC, Berkeley, and founder of the Center for Human Sleep Science—explains that preparing shortly before sleeping is, "the difference between acing an exam and failing it miserably. You cannot commit new experiences to memory if you haven't had a good night's sleep."[17] In related research, the National Sleep Foundation[18] has found that sleep synthesizes new ideas, promotes innovative thinking, and improves problem-solving abilities.

During the entire week before the interview, don't do your preparation *only* during the day. There is nothing wrong with practicing during the day, but each night just before going to sleep, review your notes or do one more walkthrough of talking points. Those memories are reactivated during the night because connections between brain cells strengthen while you are sleeping. This is turn transfers everything you've prepared from short- to long-term memory where it can be more easily accessed when needed.

Preparation is an important ingredient for having a strong interview. Time that preparation with when you go to sleep in the preceding nights and you'll maximize your odds of success when the important day arrives.

SEVEN DAYS OF SLEEP

The final step to maximizing performance is to use *the entire week* before an interview to ensure you have a regular sleep-wake cycle. The importance of the sleep-wake cycle was discovered by Swiss sleep researcher Alexander Borbély in the early 1980s. Borbély found that sleep is controlled by two processes: the circadian rhythm and sleep-wake homeostasis. Both processes control the timing of sleep and work in conjunction to regulate your body's sleep patterns. They are designed to provide you with the most effective sleep and can be improved with what experts in the field call "sleep hygiene."

Even if you achieve the right level of sleep the night before, a lack of regular sleep-wake cycle in the week preceding the interview will still interfere with the deeper sleep stages that affect memory and concentration. Finding that right balance isn't easy. Because of the hectic nature of our lives, our sleep is often misaligned with the cycles needed to maximize our mental and physical functions. According to Johns Hopkins sleep expert Dr. Rachel Salas, "Humans are essentially the only mammals that willingly deprive themselves of sleep."

To deal with this, 20 percent of adults use some method of sleep remedies (over-the-counter medicine or otherwise) to help them sleep. These remedies all interfere with cognitive functioning. Researchers at John Hopkins University instead recommend specific strategies that maximize the quality of your sleep. Their processes constitute "sleep hygiene" and are supported by a wide range of other practitioners in the field of cognitive and physical performance. Harvard Medical School,[19] Centre for Clinical Observations,[20] the Center for Disease Control,[21] and even the Gatorade Sports Science Institute[22] (which focuses on

peak performance in elite athletes) all recommend the following sleep practices to maximize performance:

1. *Don't force sleep*: If you go to bed and toss and turn for
   twenty to thirty minutes, then stop trying to sleep. Get
   out of bed and read a book or listen to relaxing music
   until you begin to feel sleepy again. Returning to bed
   at that point trains your mind to associate your bed
   with sleeping instead of struggling.
2. *Don't underestimate coffee*: Research has shown that
   consuming 400 mg of caffeine (two to three cups of
   coffee or one twenty-ounce coffee drink) six hours
   before sleeping leads to losing one hour of sleep. In the
   week preceding your interview, don't drink anything
   caffeinated six hours before going to sleep.
3. *Skip the nightcap*: Many people use alcohol to help them
   go to sleep, but it is harmful. Studies have shown that
   while alcohol can help you fall asleep faster, it reduces
   the amount of time you spend in the deep sleep stages
   that support memory and concentration.
4. *Declutter your bedroom*: Create a peaceful bedroom and
   keep it clear of clutter or anything that could serve as
   a distraction.
5. *No electronics*: Don't use any electronics thirty minutes
   before going to bed. It is darkness that helps our brain
   prepare itself for sleep. Turn off any light from your
   phone, computer, or television because it will disrupt
   your brain's internal clock.

In the week before the interview, make sure to be consistent
with this routine. Do everything you can to go to bed at the

same time each night and get up at the same time each morning, including on the weekends.*

Many people have other factors in their life that can interrupt regular sleep-wake cycles, such as having children. That is a reality. But before you discount your ability to use sleep in your favor, consider two perspectives. First, you won't be the only candidate facing circumstances that prevent adequate sleep. Second, the list of sleep hygiene practices are all completely in your control. It's an unforced error to not take the five steps suggested to get the edge you need over the candidates who don't have this knowledge.

The anxiety of heading into an interview often leads people to not only sleep less, but also sleep poorly before an interview. Knowing the research on sleep allows you to proactively address this issue. Follow a strong sleep routine in the week preceding the interview. Prepare for the interview whenever you have available time, but make sure to review your notes directly before going to sleep. Get the recommended 6.5 to 7.5 hours of sleep. Take those three steps and you'll have maximized the positive relationship between sleep and peak performance.

---

* There are an increasing number of wearable technologies that can help you monitor your sleep, including when you should go to sleep and wake.

THE FREEDOM OF PRACTICE

There is a document in the Library of Congress that contains a set of notes Abraham Lincoln wrote in the 1850s. Most historians believe they were talking points for a speech he was going to give to a group of young lawyers. The document is three pages long and in it, Lincoln advises that "extemporaneous speaking should be practiced and cultivated" because "however able and faithful (a lawyer) may be in other respects, people are slow to bring him business if he cannot make a speech."

Lincoln's advice is worth taking by anyone headed into an interview. What he is referencing with the word "extemporaneously" is the ability to speak off-the-cuff. But what he is truly advising the new lawyers on is that successfully convincing others cannot be left to chance—it must be practiced.

According to a survey[23] conducted on job applicants, 52 percent of candidates spend less than two hours researching a company and preparing for an interview.

That's right. Fifty-two percent. Less than two hours.

Once again, we see evidence of the coin toss and more reasons for the average results of interviews. Two hours is not enough. Half the people going into interviews are not prepared.

You want to clearly separate yourself from that half. Whether you land your next job will hinge on whether you practice the strategies you choose to apply from this book. Investing time to practice is what will put you ahead of your competition.

The purpose of practicing is not to memorize your answers. The purpose is to get out of your own way during the interview. The problem with interviewing is that we are often overthinking and self-conscious. We are trying to do too many things at once. Listening. Preparing an answer. Deciphering their expression. Remembering advice from this book. Trying to appear calm. Questioning ourselves. Questioning the reason for their question. Hoping we get it right. Hoping we get the job. There are too many things going on.

What you want is take some of those things off your mind during the interview. By practicing, you are removing the need—in the moment of the interview—to find the right words. Practicing isn't memorizing. Rather, it is finding the words that best convey the message—clear, concise, complete—and getting used to saying them. The patterns, the phrases, the key points. Not a script. An outline.

There has been extensive research done on how to effectively practice. In the following section, we'll focus on three specific techniques that world-class performers use when they practice.

SET SPECIFIC GOALS

D r. K. Anders Ericsson,[24] an expert in the science of expertise, has spent much of his career identifying key elements of effective practice. For over thirty years, he has studied people across domains—music, sports, chess, medicine—who are experts at what they do, to identify the practice habits that lead to strong performance. His research was featured in Malcolm Gladwell's bestseller *Outliers*, from which many people took away that you need ten thousand hours of practice to develop expertise. Ericsson has since shared that this was oversimplified and not relevant in many contexts.

In the context of interviewing, the most relevant strategy from his research is to practice with specific goals in mind. When you practice, you have to know if you are getting better. Specific goals give you direction so you can try again, notice improvement, and correct errors.

What goal should you set? You may be inclined to believe the goal should be giving strong answers. But you need to be more specific, the goal is the *strong delivery* of an answer. This nuance is important because you won't always have a strong answer, even when you prepare well. You will have foundations for strong answers. Some will match questions perfectly, some will be counteroffers, some won't match as well as you'd like.

But the delivery of the answer can influence how well the answer lands. The goal is to practice *giving* your answers really well. Practice allows you to get used to the words you will use. A well-delivered answer, with content that is slightly off the mark, will beat an answer that has the right content but is delivered poorly.

So far, the goal is "strong delivery of an answer." According to Ericsson's research, that still isn't specific enough. To improve the goal, let's recall the ideal length of an answer and add that to the goal.

Now the goal is "strong delivery of an answer in two to three minutes."

That is exactly the type of goal you need for interview practice. You will know if you've gone too long or too short. You'll start to get a feel for what two to three minutes feels like. Equally as important, you'll get a feel for how much information you can put inside that time frame.

The first time you practice an answer, don't time it. Just get the words out. Do that several times without timing it. You're not memorizing, you just want to find the right words that naturally emerge from you. Once you've identified the general answer, then figure out how you want to structure it. Logic? Story? Both? Play around with structure to determine what fits best. Then time yourself.

You will probably initially go over three minutes. That's fine, because now comes the next step—pruning. You want to give an answer that gets to the core of your point relatively quickly. Since you have a time limit, determine what elements of your answer need to be cut entirely. Start pruning the answer to the main elements that convey your message. The leaner the answer, the more you will realize that practice isn't about committing a speech to memory. It is about identifying your main talking points and letting those tumble out of you organically when the question is asked.

PRACTICE IN DIFFERENT MEDIUMS

O nce you've identified your key talking points within the two- to three-minute frame, it's time to consider *where* to practice. Your interview will likely be at a table or desk. There will likely be one or two people facing you. Beyond that, you'll have very little information on the environment in which you'll interview. What you don't want to do is practice in the same setting over and over because you will get accustomed to that space. Once you leave it, you will struggle to naturally provide answers because you won't have the physical or spatial cues to help remind you of your main points.

To overcome this, practice in different places and practice both in your head and out loud. Elite athletes will often rehearse a movement mentally. They will visualize it with extreme detail. You should do the same for your answers. Rather than speaking out loud, sometimes just think through your talking points. In some ways, this is a different medium, a different place—in your mind—that you are practicing.

But you also need to hear yourself saying the words. Imagining what you will say, and actually saying it out loud are two different activities. Practice in your head, but also do it out loud. Practicing out loud lets you stumble through wording and timing in a way that mentally rehearsing cannot do. You want to feel the rhythm and cadence of what you will say as much as the content. Those are the mechanisms that allow your mind to capture those moments and then naturally bring them back out during the interview.

Practice in your car as you drive to work. Practice in your living room. Then in your bedroom. Take a walk and talk through some answers. Practice in your backyard, balcony, or front porch. Keep switching it up. You want the outline of your main points to live in you, not in any particular context you consistently practice in. That changing of medium allows the answer you generate to be transportable to the interview room regardless of what that happens to look like.

OUT OF ORDER AND BROKEN UP

A wide range of experts have studied how top professionals practice. Two of those experts are professor Dr. Annie Bosler and peak performance psychologist Dr. Don Greene. Bosler and Greene have found that frequent repetition with allotted breaks is the most common habit of practice found across elite performers.[25]

In other words, don't practice interviewing for an entire hour. That is suboptimal because that leads to memorizing. If you practice for an hour at a time, you will find yourself getting used to answering certain questions in a certain order. You will be less nimble with the underlying content. Then in the actual interview, when the questions are asked in a different order or phrased differently than you expected, you will suddenly find yourself out of place.

Instead, break up your practice. Split your practice time into small, concentrated chunks and work on them at different times each day.* Focus on three questions you want to practice answering. Do several repetitions answering those. Then take a break. Do something completely different. Come back to the practice session later and practice a different set of three. Alternate what three answers you bundle together for practice.

Remember that you simply want to get the timing down and get the words out. You want to get used to the ideas and outline. You want to feel the rhythm of the talking points.

---

* Keep in mind the research on how preparing before you sleep improves your performance. That doesn't mean you should only practice in the evenings. Practice whenever you have time. But review your notes shortly before sleeping to help lock them in.

Those are the main benefits you are trying to gain from practice. Repetition with breaks allows you to do that extremely well.

LANDING A JOB DURING A CRISIS:
THE NEW ABNORMAL

Just as I was completing the final draft of this book, COVID-19 began to tear through communities across the world, taking the economy hostage along the way. China, Italy, and Spain were initially the hardest hit, with each responding by locking down their countries. By March of 2020, one-third of the world was in some form of lockdown. In that same month, the World Health Organization officially declared the outbreak a pandemic and the US declared it a national emergency. By early April, roughly 95 percent of all Americans were under lockdown as forty-two states issued stay-at-home orders. By mid-April, over 22 million Americans had filed for unemployment.[26]

News about COVID-19 was whipsawing the nation with each headline and social media post: Don't wear face masks. Wear face masks. The elderly are vulnerable. The young are vulnerable. This will end soon. This will be seasonal. We knew this was coming. No one knew this was coming. We're overreacting. We're underreacting. The market is down. Now it's up. Now it's down.

One truth that became readily apparent was that when a crisis of this magnitude happens, it takes a while before things return to normal. As the situation evolves, people try to adjust to "the new normal." But that rarely means much because a day later, everything changes. Then everyone says that's the new normal . . . until the next day.

The truth is, during a crisis, today is abnormal and tomorrow will only bring a new abnormal. That doesn't mean we stop looking forward. It does mean that when abnormal doesn't yet have an end date, you must accept that things will be unpredictable. You must expect randomness. You must be prepared for an economic impact that will likely stretch beyond the eventual flattening of the curve for that particular crisis.

People and economies do gradually heal. But in the tougher moments, genuine support for one other is vital. That includes providing guidance to those with disrupted career paths. When you search the internet for such advice, you'll find a consistent set of themes:

- Update and/or revamp your resume and LinkedIn profile
- Expand and tap into your network
- Take online courses and learn new skills
- Be patient and persistent

This is all great advice worth taking—but it isn't enough. The strategies found in this book are now more relevant than ever. The importance of putting yourself in the shoes of employers and understanding how they think is essential to career success. Landing the job you deserve means you need to know what will drive their hiring decisions when the future is hazy. Most importantly, you need to know what that means for you as you interact with them.

This chapter and the next were written with that mind. They don't fit neatly into one of the "power" chapters. But given the unique situation we are in—and that this won't be the last crisis we'll need to navigate—the chapters felt important to add.

Employers need people who can pivot
During a crisis, organizations need to be agile and adaptable—which aren't the same thing. Normally, organizations

can adapt, and evolve over time. But to survive uncertainty, they must also be agile because no one is sure what's coming next. "Agile" means that leaders can change quickly *within* the boundaries of their existing organization. To accomplish that, they need people who can execute at high levels and pivot when things change.

That means during job interviews, you want to share examples of when you changed course on short notice. That type of pivot requires comfort with ambiguity. If you need lots of information, high amounts of clarity, or a very hands-on manager—this is not the time to show that. This is the time to demonstrate (and develop) your ability to advance work despite uncertainty. Be prepared to answer questions like:

- "Have you had to adjust to changes over which you had no control? How did you handle it?"
- "What do you do when priorities change quickly? Share an example."
- "Do you have an example of adapting to a wide variety of situations or environments?"

Employers need people who can plug and play
During the COVID-19 crisis, the number of people working remotely skyrocketed. That will either stay high or come down only to shoot up again with another outbreak. Given shifts in both technology and desired flexibility by workers, this type of fluctuation will become commonplace. In addition, crises often create environments in which team members may leave work for extended periods of time because they or a family member are incapacitated in some way.

The term "plug and play" is used to describe devices that work perfectly as soon as they are connected. You don't need to become a robot to land a job, but you do need to recognize that people who can easily play more than one position—either in terms of function or physical space—will be highly valued.

- On your resume and during the interview, indicate you are set-up to work from home. Show familiarity with some type of videoconferencing (Zoom, Skype, etc.). Do the same for collaborative tools (Slack, Asana, etc.). If you aren't familiar with them, find one with a free trial and get comfortable with its functionality.
- Give examples of times you have taken on work that was not yours, backfilled an open role, or otherwise stepped outside your position. Pinch-hitting is a unique skill. Employers will want people who have expertise in their current role and can move into different roles if necessary.

Employers don't want to worry about productivity

As how (and where) we work changes, it will become more complex for managers to measure productivity. Whether it is because everyone's role is shifting or because managing remote teams is new to them—managers will struggle with knowing who is doing what. Don't give them reason to worry.

- Give examples that show, with absolute clarity, that you accomplish whatever is asked of you. Begin answers by saying, "I was asked to do _____." Then give a bit of context, explain what you did, and end with, "And we accomplished exactly what was asked . . ." Don't leave room for any doubt about your ability to execute.
- Think of examples that demonstrate a can-do attitude, optimism, and strong time-management. Focus on your ability to communicate upward and outward, always keeping relevant people informed of your work and progress. Managers will have many things on their

mind and removing the concern of having to monitor you closely will be important.

Employers will want a different type of manager

During recessions, crises, or other times of uncertainty, organizations are often hesitant to hire full-time staff. A primary driver of this is their need to remain flexible. Another driver, equally as important, is that reductions in force are stressful. No one wants to lay off their co-workers. In order to stay agile and avoid the turmoil of letting people go, organizations often hire temporary staff, part-time staff, consultants, or contractors.

The other factor that had been gaining momentum and bolted to the forefront in 2020 was the necessity to shift to remote work and teams connected only by technology. A study[27] by Owl Labs found that, globally, 56 percent of organizations allow remote work. While this is more than half, the same study found only 16 percent of those organizations are fully remote. So leading a fully remote team is still far from the norm for most managers.

Managing flexible staffing models is different than managing full-time employees. Managing people in the same physical setting is different than when they are all remote. If you are seeking a new management role, you need to be prepared to demonstrate that you can manage all sides of this evolving, revolving coin.

If you have led teams in either scenario, make sure to include examples to demonstrate your experience with that type of management. If you haven't, keep in mind the following key elements and do further research so you are prepared to demonstrate success in each context.

Managing remote teams

Remote teams face a unique set of common challenges such as communication breakdowns, decreased motivation, lack of personal connection, and ineffective ways to measure productivity. To overcome this, strong managers of remote teams demonstrate the following characteristics:

- They understand that effectively measuring productivity requires clarity of goals, aligned expectations, and a focus on monitoring goals and results versus monitoring time on task.
- They aren't as rigid about *when* people work. They recognize that working from home doesn't necessarily align with the traditional nine-to-five schedule. This may occur because people live in different time zones or because they have different circumstances in their home. However . . .
- . . . they do establish clear "rules of engagement," such as certain days and times when group work occurs, guidelines for email responsiveness, certain times when no calls are allowed, etc.
- They have a strong familiarity with videoconferencing technology (Skype, Zoom, etc.) and collaborative tools (Slack, Asana, etc.).
- They conduct check-ins and meetings that aren't only focused on work, i.e., they make sure to build trust, connect on a personal level, and create space for levity (gifs, memes, emoticons, etc.).

Managing flexible employees

An important thing to note is that managing flexible employees does have similarities to managing full-time employees. The element of time, however, creates important shifts in your approach. You will have less time to get to know team members in a flexible staffing model and they have less time to get things done. In many ways, this requires similar skills as those mentioned for remote workers. A few additional ones are worth noting about strong managers.

- They treat part-time workers, contractors and consultants with the same respect as full-time workers. They include them in relevant meetings, give them feedback and make themselves accessible.
- They spend time getting to know their career desires and are clear about whether career advancement is possible in their current role. Regardless of career opportunities, they provide opportunities for flexible employees to grow and develop as professionals.
- They make them feel like they are part of the bigger picture. Just because they are on contract or consulting doesn't mean they don't have a desire to understand the vision and larger strategy, which helps keep them motivated and engaged.
- They don't forget to thank them for their contributions and show gratitude. Employees who aren't full-time are often forgotten during celebrations or recognitions. But those moments are just as important for their motivation and sense of impact as anyone else.

A Unique Skill

Some of this advice may feel as though you'll become a widget to be inserted anywhere and expected to execute and produce. That would be a misinterpretation. While I cannot predict how your employer will manage you, I can assure you that your ability to be effective during uncertainty is a powerful skill that requires self-awareness, quick learning, responsiveness, and relationship building. Even with an average manager as your boss, these competencies will give you more independence and autonomy than those without them.

The people making hiring decisions are human too. Unexpected situations, personal and professional, will be weighing on their hearts and minds. Position yourself as one less thing to be concerned about. Be the embodiment of the stability we all need. Keep this advice in mind during your job search and you'll inspire the confidence and competence required to collectively fight our way to a better tomorrow.

PHONE AND VIDEO INTERVIEWS: THE NEW NORMAL

Let's start with a few facts. Of US workers, 3.6 percent work from home half of the time or more.[1] That's a relatively low percentage. But if you swing the lens to the percentage of US employees who have jobs in which they *could* work from home if needed—that number jumps significantly. A study done at the Becker Friedman Institute for Economics at the University of Chicago found that 37 percent of jobs could be performed entirely at home.[2] A similar study done by Global Workplace Analytics (GWA) found that number to be 56 percent.[3] Those jobs include, among other things, work that can be done individually versus in a group, roles that don't require personal contact with customers, and jobs not requiring physical work that needs to be done on-site. In the gap between the current number of people working from home and those that could if needed, you can see the future direction of work.

That future came crashing into the present with the COVID-19 pandemic. Due to increasing concerns about the rapid spread of the virus, social distancing, and a need to "flatten the curve" so hospitals wouldn't be overrun with patients, large portions of the economy shut down overnight. Many organizations with employees who could work from home quickly shifted to remote working conditions.

The comfort with remote work and the belief that people not only could, but should, work from home is taking a dramatic turn. According to GWA, by 2021 the percent of the US workforce working remotely multiple days a week will jump from 3.6 percent, to between 25 and 30 percent.[4]

This shift not only impacts the current workforce, but also how workers will be hired. Phone interviews and video interviews will become increasingly popular. That may occur because once organizations are accustomed to remote work, the need to meet people face-to-face for hiring decisions will become less important. Or, it may be driven by health concerns, COVID-19 or otherwise, that push organizations to hire people without physically interacting with them.

This may all seem overblown or unrealistic. But, if you search for statistics on the number of organizations who use video conferencing for hiring, you'll find that roughly 60 percent of organizations do video interviews and another 22 percent would consider it.[5] Pandemic or not, the odds that you will have to do a phone or video interview are high and will only increase.

It is in your best interest to be prepared for both.

The Phone Interview

Phone interviews generally occur early in the hiring process and are used either as a short screening process or as a substitute for an in-person interview. If their primary purpose is as a screen, then they are a tool to efficiently weed out candidates. Anyone who has served as an interviewer has done an in-person interview in which they identified significant concerns that could have been identified through a brief phone screen, thereby saving valuable time. Avoiding those moments is why organizations do phone screens. If the phone interview is replacing an in-person interview, it is usually because the candidate is in another city and the organization is reluctant to pay for a flight early in the process.

Regardless of the purpose, your approach is the same—prepare for them both as you would an in-person interview, including the use of strategies from this book. Then focus on a few points of differentiation mentioned below, each with practices to consider and unforced errors to avoid.

Using notes during the interview
Since the interviewer can't see you, your impulse will be to have notes in front of you. That is a good idea, but the error most people make is having too many notes. You want to prepare for a phone interview as though you are preparing for an in-person interview. If you've prepared correctly, then the primary item you need in front of you is your resume.

Your resume has been built around stories and experiences that you can share. It is fine to jot some additional high-level talking points on the resume to help jog your memory. But what you want to avoid is having countless notes on index cards or sheets of paper scattered around your computer or taped to the wall in front of you. This will be a distraction. Your energy will go toward finding the "right" answer and then trying to read that answer naturally. Instead, focus your attention on your resume and the stories you can pull from there. Odds are high they are looking at that same resume on their end and your answers will align with what they are reading.

In addition to your resume, you can have a short set of notes on background information about the organization, the role and the team you are interviewing to join. Those notes should be in large print and in bullet form. You do not want a transcript you have to read. You want a road map of things that are important because they are tied to their story and might not come to mind because they aren't tied as closely to your story. Key elements to gather include:

- The size of the organization in terms of people and budget
- Their strategies and any challenges they have been facing

- Core principles, values and/or mission statement
- Team responsibilities and role responsibilities
- Why this role/team is interesting to you

That is all you need in front of you. Your resume. High-level talking points. And no more than one page with the key elements about the hiring organization. That allows you to have enough information to prime an answer, but not so much that you are mentally distracted by searching for information on papers in front of you instead of listening and answering questions naturally.

They can't see you . . . but pretend they can
Since the interviewer cannot see you, it may seem odd to discuss what you should physically be doing during a phone interview. Research, however, suggests otherwise. Humans are constantly picking up social cues from each other, and some of them come through your voice. A study[6] from the Yale University School of Management found that while people learn a lot about you by reading your facial expressions, they can read *even more* from your voice alone. Therefore, you want to do as much as possible to help your voice send the right cues.

That means although you maybe in the comfort of your own home, you still want to dress the part. Follow the same rules from the chapter on how to dress. If the organization is a place where you'd wear a suit to interview in-person, then wear a suit for the phone interview. If the dress is casual attire, then dress that way as well, but one notch higher. Remember this isn't just about managing their impression. How you dress also positively impacts how you think and how you perceive yourself, which still matters by phone.

The advice in previous chapters about expansive body and gestures also applies in this setting. Since the interviewer can't see you, confidence and competence must come through your voice. Do the exercise in which you thrust your hands into the air as though you've just scored a victory. Use the exercise where you put your hands out, palms up and point your thumbs back to open your chest. During the interview, don't sit. Stand and make gestures as though you were in person.

During a phone interview, how well you communicate has heightened importance because there are less cues for the interviewer to interpret. As a result, how well you communicate isn't just used to assess your communication skills but becomes a proxy for your talent in general. If you communicate well and with confidence, that will have a strong positive impact on whether the interviewer thinks you have the skills they need.

Smile

A final word of advice on the physical side of the phone interview is to smile occasionally during the interview. Research[7] has shown that when you smile, even a fake smile, your stress decreases, and the way you think and feel improves. That same energy will come through to the interviewer in your voice.

If the idea of smiling to yourself during an interview feels forced, then try another strategy. Before you begin the interview, hold a pencil between your teeth horizontally and don't let your lips touch the pencil. By placing a pencil across your mouth, you are forcing the corners of your mouth to go up, like a smile. Studies in which participants performed this activity, showed that this triggered the same feelings in them as a smile. This is known as facial feedback hypothesis[8] and it suggests the way you feel can be influenced by your facial expression even when your expression did not result from an emotional experience.

It worth noting that most job opportunities begin with a phone call of some sort. Whether it's an introductory call, phone screen, or formal interview—don't underestimate the importance of that initial impression. Phones are not a medium we generally associate with assessment and it is easy to under-prepare. Being proactive and thoughtful about how you use the phone interview gives you an edge over candidates who view it more traditionally and therefore less strategically.

Video Interviews
Like phone interviews, video interviews are a cost-effective way to do begin the hiring process while capturing some of the benefits of an in-person interview. Although video can't repli-cate meeting someone in person, it does allow increased inter-personal connection with the candidate. In this way, they are better than phone interviews because the interviewer is more likely to pick up on social cues that improve assessment of more nuanced skills and attributes.

Because video interviews are similar to in-person inter-views in terms of visual cues, many of the same strategies should be used, but with a few twists to accommodate for the technology.

Dress the part
By now, the science of dressing should be clear. You'll be tempted to be a bit more casual. Resist that temptation. If you would have worn a suit to a meeting in their organization, then do the same by video. If they are doing the interview from work, they will be dressed for work—and you should too.

Computer at eye level
Eye contact during video interviews is interesting because it doesn't actually happen. The entire value of eye contact is the ability to look directly at someone and engage in a uniquely human way. Technology automatically creates distance and

can't recreate true eye contact. You can, however, take several steps to shorten that distance, or at a minimum, not expand it.

Position your computer so the camera is at eye level. If that requires you to place it on a stack of books, then do so. It may look odd to you, but the interviewer won't know what you've done. What they will know is whether you are looking directly into the camera. If you don't do this, the camera will either be too high or too low and the interview will feel like you are either looking down or looking up the entire time. That's unnatural and creates a disconnect that you can't afford to leave in place.

Look into the camera . . . not at yourself

During a video interview, the image of the interviewer will be on the screen in front of you. But you will also have a small video of yourself inset in one of the corners of your screen. Throughout the interview it will be hard to resist the temptation to look at yourself either periodically or for the duration of the call. This distracts from your ability to focus on the interviewer. It also distracts from you looking into the camera because it appears that you are looking to the side.

If there is a function for removing that inset, then remove it. If not, then simply cover it with a piece of tape in advance. It can be difficult to not look at yourself during an interview, either because you want to ensure you look appropriate or simply because you don't see yourself on video that often. It will draw your attention from focusing on the interviewer and the questions they are asking. To make things worse, research[9] shows when you look at yourself, you will likely be disappointed by what you see. This may be due to a bias called "self-enhancement" in which we think we appear better than we do—until we see ourselves. This isn't a cognitive function you want triggered in a moment when the goal is to confidently present your best self.

Minimize distractions

In previous chapters, the importance of keeping your resume free of distractions was discussed. The same rule applied when it came to how you should dress during the interview. No surprise, this is equally important for video interviews. On video, however, interviewers are not distracted by you as much as they are by what appears in your background.

When you set up your camera find a location where there isn't anything in the background that will draw the interviewer's attention away from you and what you are discussing. If you are at home, they don't need to see what your couch looks like, nor your kitchen. The less there is going on behind you, the better. Whenever possible, sit facing a window, otherwise light will shine into the camera from behind you and you will appear to be tucked into a deep shadow.

Some video conferencing technology has a functionality that will blur your background, if so—use it. There is also functionality that lets you choose your background from an array of graphics. Be careful with those. While they do have professional backdrops which you could use (e.g., an office setting), sometimes you also end up being cropped or even chopped by the software.

Having done countless video interviews, I can tell you that interviewers do notice items in the background. Technology may be advancing, but the people watching are human, with all our cognitive flaws still in place. It is hard not to judge the background a candidate chooses to share without it somehow impacting judgement of the candidate themselves.

Test your technology

This easily falls into the category of unforced errors, which means it needs to be briefly mentioned. Test out your camera to make sure both the video and audio are working and that the signal is strong. Have a friend or family member call you and report back on how you sound and look. If possible, do this in the physical location you plan to use so you know the strength of the signal and can find a different location if needed. As mentioned above, get comfortable with the various functionalities.

Technology malfunctioning isn't something you have to worry about during an in-person interview. But to drive this point home, imagine if you walked into an interview room and suddenly lost your voice. That would create an immediate disconnect. Even when your voice returned, that odd experience would still impact the experience, and not for the better. The same happens via video. If they can't hear you or if the signal drops, you will be trying to fix it frantically on your end—burning positive energy. On their end, consciously or subconsciously, it will affect how competent you seem.

Get ahead of this by testing your technology. In addition, at the start of the interview ask them if you can share your cell phone number with them, in case you get disconnected. While the odds are low you'll run into these issues, the odds are high that if you do, they will impact the experience. Those are the odds you're managing, so that in an unexpected moment, your forward momentum doesn't slow.

Your North Star
When the hiring environment changes, whether due to a crisis or otherwise, your North Star maintains its importance—a personalized strategy that helps you succeed during your next interview. The path to success has never been linear. Pivots always happen. In some hiring environments they happen harder and more frequently. In those times, when it is unclear

where the pendulum will finally rest, keep identifying the areas you can control and leveraging the power you have. Most importantly, continue being authentic about who you are, truthful about what you can do, and incredibly strategic about how you present those things.

AFTERWORD

The belief that interviewers are in control has been seared into our minds from our earliest moments. We have been conditioned to believe that the person asking questions, and demanding answers, is the person in charge. That's what we've been told from the first moment we sat on a rug listening to our kindergarten teacher. That experience continues every day until we graduate from high school. For those who go to college, it is further reinforced there as well. By the time we are eventually being interviewed for jobs—whether it is for a summer job, an internship, or our first job out of college—that perception is engrained in us, and only deepens as we progress through our careers.

This perception isn't only seared into the mind of the candidate. It is seared into the mind of the interviewer. They believe they are in control. Everything that happens in the interview room, happens on their terms. The questions they ask. The pace of the interview. The tone they set. The location. The time of day. The rules by which you will engage. The expectations they have. All of it on their terms.

But this book calls into question whether it all really is under their control. Certainly, what occurs after the interview is in their hands. But that is heavily influenced by what happens at the interview table. I've spent many years on the interviewer side of that table and have realized there are fewer things under my control than there appear to be. My position of control is a well-maintained illusion, until I find myself in front of a candidate who knows what they are doing. Then I've seen how easy it is for the tables to turn. In those moments I'm not making a decision about the candidate. Instead, a decision is getting made for me—by the candidate.

The word "candidate" has an interesting origin story, one that is rooted in power. It began as a political term. The word "*candidus*" means "white" in Latin. In ancient Rome, when a person ran for a position of power, they wore a toga whitened with chalk. *Candidus* symbolized honesty, sincerity, spontaneity, forthrightness, and eventually became the word "candid." It is no surprise that those same traits are what interviewers want from candidates during an interview. To make the right hiring decision, we need them to be candid. We need them to guide us to the truth.

And that is how the tables turn. That is how the candidate becomes empowered.

The only person who knows if you are the right person for the job is you. To gain that knowledge, we have to go through you. We have no other option. That gives you—the candidate—a tremendous amount of power. You are not the student on the rug. You are the teacher. You are educating the interviewer about who you are, what you can do, and why they should hire you.

The strategies in this book are about using that power and giving you control. The strategies give you a deeper understanding of yourself. They provide an inside perspective on how interviewers think, so you have a better understanding of them as well. The *entrevue* is never one-sided. It is an interaction in which you have influence. Don't give that power away. If you do, your odds of success will be the same as everyone else—50 percent.

Instead, identify the strategies that suit your context and use them to take control. Information, intention, and preparation always shift the odds in your favor. And once you recognize the power you have, you will land the job you deserve. You will build toward the future you've envisioned for yourself. You won't just be able to pay the bills today, you'll have work that provides fulfillment across many years.

ACKNOWLEDGMENTS

For Oralia. For my parents, brothers, sister, and children. For anyone who wants a better life, an opportunity to do great things, or just a chance to move forward.

The word "hustle" has many definitions; to achieve by energetic activity . . . to urge forward . . . to make strenuous efforts to obtain money or business . . . to play a sport in an alert, aggressive manner. Each meaning is slightly different, but all speak to the spirit with which you pursue a goal.

"Hustle," in the way I will use it here, has that same spirit. Hustle means to vigorously pursue a better position in life. I would not be here without hustle. Nor would I be here had I not learned it from others. To them I owe thanks.

To my older brother who did it, often at personal risk, to support his family. To my younger brother who does it through creative pursuits. To my sister who proves it can be done while balancing creativity and family. To my nieces and nephews, who are cut from the same cloth. To my father for refusing to work for anyone. To my mother for starting her life over at forty-eight. To my wife for going to graduate school and motivating me to do the same. To her parents, whose inspiring story of immigration embodies it. To Deena Williams Mangrum and Eleisha Nelson-Reed for demonstrating it can be done while having full-time careers. To Jeremy Levitt and Paul Williams for being with me when I was in the middle of it, and for showing me how to change lanes. To the Burrell and the James families for supporting me in my youth, because no one moves forward alone.

NOTES

Introduction
1. Frank L. Schmidt and John E. Hunter. "The Validity and Utility of Selection Methods in Personnel Psychology: Practical and Theoretical Implications of 85 years of Research Findings." *Psychological Bulletin* 124, no. 2 (1998): 262–274.
2. Randall J. Beck and Jim Carter. "Why Great Managers Are So Rare." Gallup. https://www.gallup.com/workplace/231593/why-great-managers-rare.aspx.
3. US Department of Labor, Bureau of Labor Statistics. https://www.bls.gov/news.release/tenure.nr0.htm.

The Eleven Powers
1. Pamela Babcock. "Spotting Lies." *SHRM HR Magazine*. (October 1, 2003).
2. Charles F. Bond, Jr., and Bella M. DePaulo. "Accuracy of Deception Judgments." *Personality and Social Psychology Review* 10, no. 3 (August 1, 2006): 214–234.

Section One
1. The Ladders. "Eye Tracking Study." http://go.theladders.com/rs/539-NBG-120/images/EyeTracking-Study.pdf.
2. Dean Buonomano. *Your Brain is a Time Machine*. W. W. Norton & Company. (2017).
3. Michael Kearney. "Persuading Audiences with Statistical Evidence." (2014). Available at https://www.researchgate.net/publication/322819700_Persuading_Audiences_with_Statistical_Evidence.

4. Daniel M. Cable. "Striving for Self-Verification During Organizational Entry." (2012). Available at https://pdfs. semanticscholar.org/9e30/5691bb1d5c2d86dc23ffe5b2627 7143a93fe.pdf.

5. Adam M. Grant, Francesca Gino, and David A. Hofmann. "Reversing the Extraverted Leadership Advantage: The Role of Employee Proactivity." *Academy of Management Journal* 54, no. 3 (2011). Available at https://doi.org/10.5465/ amj.2011.61968043.

6. Matt Abrahams. "Think Fast, Talk Smart: Communication Techniques." YouTube. Uploaded by Stanford Graduate School of Business. December 4, 2014. Available at www. youtube.com/watch?v=HAnw168huqA.

7. Hyunjin Song. "The Effects of Processing Fluency on Judgment and Processing Style." (2009). Available at https:// deepblue.lib.umich.edu/bitstream/handle/2027.42/63625/ hyunjins_1.pdf?sequence=1.

8. Deanne L. Westerman, Meredith Lanska, and Justin M. Olds. "The Effect of Processing Fluency on Impressions of Familiarity and Liking." *Journal of Experimental Psychology: Learning, Memory, and Cognition* 41, no. 2 (2015): 426–438.

9. Maria Konnikova. "A List of Reasons Why Our Brains Love Lists." *The New Yorker.* December 2, 2013.

10. Fritz Heider and Marianne Simmel. "An Experimental Study of Apparent Behavior." *The American Journal of Psychology* 57 (1944): 243–259.

11. Vanessa Boris. "What Makes Storytelling So Effective for Learning?" Harvard Business Publishing. (December 20, 2017). Available at https://www.harvardbusiness.org/ what-makes-storytelling-so-effective-for-learning/.

12. Hyunjin Song. "The Effects of Processing Fluency on Judgment and Processing Style." (2009). Available at https://

deepblue.lib.umich.edu/bitstream/handle/2027.42/63625/
hyunjins_1.pdf?sequence=1.

13. Barak Rosenshine. "Principles of Instruction: Research-
Based Strategies That All Teachers Should Know."
American Educator 36, no. 1 (2012): 12–19.

14. Matthew A. Killingsworth and Daniel T. Gilbert. "A
Wandering Mind Is an Unhappy Mind." *Science* 330, no.
6006 (November 12, 2010): 932.

15. Peter R. Killeen. "Absent Without Leave; A Neuroenergetic
Theory of Mind Wandering." *Frontiers in Psychology*
(July 1, 2013). Available at https://doi.org/10.3389/
fpsyg.2013.00373.

16. This Week in Tech. *Tech News Today* 1418. "Holiday
Special – Sherry Turkle." (December 30 2015). Available at
https://twit.tv/shows/tech-news-today/episodes/1418.

17. Andrew K. Przybylski and Netta Weinstein. "Can You
Connect with Me Now? How the Presence of Mobile
Communication Technology Influences Face-to-Face
Conversation Quality." *Journal of Social and Personal
Relationships.* (July 19, 2012). Available at https://doi.
org/10.1177/0265407512453827.

18. Bill Thornton, Alyson Faires, Maija Robbins, and Eric Rollins.
"The Mere Presence of a Cell Phone May be Distracting:
Implications for Attention and Task Performance." *Social
Psychology* 45, no. 6 (November 2014): 479–488.

19. Jessica S. Mendoza, Benjamin C. Pody, Seungyeon Lee,
Minsung Kim, and Ian M. McDonough. "The Effect of
Cellphones on Attention and Learning: The Influences
of Time, Distraction, and Nomophobia." *Computers in
Human Behavior* 86 (April 2018): 52–60.

20. Adrian F. Ward, Kristen Duke, Ayelet Gneezy, and
Maarten W. Bos. "Brain Drain: The Mere Presence of
One's Own Smartphone Reduces Available Cognitive

Capacity." *Journal of the Association for Consumer Research* 2, no. 2 (April 2017): 140–154.

Section Two

1. Magda B. L. Donia, Gary Johns, and Usman Raja. "Good Soldier or Good Actor? Supervisor Accuracy in Distinguishing Between Selfless and Self-Serving OCB Motives." *Journal of Business and Psychology* 31, no. 1 (March 2016): 23–32.
2. Darren C. Treadway, Gerald R. Ferris, Allison B. Duke, Garry L. Adams, and Jason B. Thatcher. "The Moderating Role of Subordinate Political Skill on Supervisors' Impressions of Subordinate Ingratiation and Ratings of Subordinate Interpersonal Facilitation." *Journal of Applied Psychology* 92, no. 3 (2007): 848–855.
3. Elaine Chan and Jaideep Sengupta. "Insincere Flattery Actually Works: A Dual Attitudes Perspective." *Journal of Marketing Research* 47, no. 1 (February 2010): 122–133.
4. B.J. Fogg and Clifford Nass. "Silicon Sycophants: The Effects of Computers that Flatter." *International Journal of Human–Computer Studies* 46, no. 5 (May 1997): 551–561.
5. Elaine Chan and Jaideep Sengupta. "Observing Flattery: A Social Comparison Perspective." *Journal of Consumer Research* 40, no. 4 (December 2013): 740–758.
6. Alison Wood Brooks and Leslie K. John. "The Surprising Power of Questions." *Harvard Business Review.* (May/June 2018).
7. Alison Wood Brooks and Leslie K. John. "The Surprising Power of Questions." *Harvard Business Review.* (May/June 2018).
8. Karen Huang, Michael Yeomans, Alison Wood Brooks, Julia Minson, and Francesca Gino. "It Doesn't Hurt to Ask:

Question-Asking Increases Liking." *Journal of Personality and Social Psychology* 113, no. 3 (2017): 430–452.

9. Naoaki Kawakami, Tadashi Kikuchi, and Fujio Yoshida. "Generalization of the Mere Exposure Effect Through Peculiarity of Handwriting." *Japanese Journal of Social Psychology* 29, no. 3 (2014): 187–193.

10. Chip Heath and Amos Tversky. "Preference and Belief: Ambiguity and Competence in Choice Under Uncertainty." *Journal of Risk and Uncertainty* 4. (January 1991): 5–28.

11. Gur Huberman. "Familiarity Breeds Investment." *The Review of Financial Studies* 14, no. 3 (July 1, 2001): 659–680.

Section Three

1. Mark R. Leary and Robin M. Kowalski. "Impression Management: A literature Review and Two-Component Model." *Psychological Bulletin* 107, no. 1 (1990): 34–47.

2. Caroline F. Keating. "Why and How the Silent Self Speaks Volumes: Functional Approaches to Nonverbal Impression Management." In Valerie Manusov and Miles L. Patterson (Eds.), *The SAGE Handbook of Nonverbal Communication.* (2006): 321–339.

3. Rebecca Vickers. *Nonverbal Communication in the Employment Interview: Gender Differences in Impression Management Techniques.* (2006). Available at https://pdfs. semanticscholar.org/3ff8/1b0f95afd226742e9292b05afff8 3e7977f9.pdf.

4. Judee K. Burgoon and Norah E. Dunbar. "Nonverbal Expressions of Dominance and Power in Human Relationships." In Valerie Manusov and Miles L. Patterson (Eds.), *The SAGE Handbook of Nonverbal Communication.* (2006): 279–297.

5. Jessica L. Tracy and David Matsumoto. "The Spontaneous Expression of Pride and Shame: Evidence for Biologically Innate Nonverbal Displays." *Proceedings of the National Academy of Sciences of the United States of America* 105, no. 33 (August 19, 2008): 11,655–11,660.
6. Shwetha Nair, Mark Sagar, John J. Sollers, Nathan S. Consedine, Elizabeth Broadbent. "Do Slumped and Upright Postures Affect Stress Responses? A Randomized Trial." *Health Psychology* 34, no. 6 (June 2015): 632–641.
7. Neil Howlett, Karen Pine, Ismail Orakçıoğlu, and Ben Fletcher. "The Influence of Clothing on First Impressions: Rapid and Positive Responses to Minor Changes in Male Attire." *Journal of Fashion Marketing and Management* 17 (February 22, 2013): 38–48.
8. Dorothy U. Behling and Elizabeth A. Williams. "Influence of Dress on Perception of Intelligence and Expectations of Scholastic Achievement." *Clothing and Textiles Research Journal* 9, no. 4 (June 1, 1991): 1–7.
9. Michael L. Slepian, Simon N. Ferber, Joshua M. Gold, and Abraham M. Rutchick. "The Cognitive Consequences of Formal Clothing." *Social Psychological and Personality Science* 6, no. 6 (August 1, 2015): 661–668.
10. Hajo Adam and Adam D. Galinsky. "Enclothed Cognition." *Journal of Experimental Social Psychology* 48, no. 4 (July 2012): 918–925.
11. Judith E. Glaser and Richard D. Glaser. "The Neurochemistry of Positive Conversations." *Harvard Business Review*. (June 12, 2014).
12. Gerben A. Van Kleef. "How Emotions Regulate Social Life: The Emotions as Social Information (EASI) Model." *Current Directions in Psychological Science* 18, no. 3 (June 1, 2009): 184–188.

13. Elizabeth Scott. "How to Reframe Situations so They Create Less Stress." VeryWellMind. (April 1, 2020). Available at https://www.verywellmind.com/cognitive-reframing-for-stress-management-3144872.

14. Matthew D. Lieberman, Naomi I. Eisenberger, Molly J. Crockett, Sabrina M. Tom, Jennifer H. Pfeifer, and Baldwin M. Way. "Putting Feelings Into Words." *Psychological Science* 18, no. 5 (May 1, 2007): 421–428.

15. Andrea N. Niles, Michelle G. Craske, Matthew D. Lieberman, and Christopher Hur. "Affect Labeling Enhances Exposure Effectiveness for Public Speaking Anxiety." *Behaviour Research and Therapy* 68 (March 2015): 27–36.

16. Kitty Klein and Adriel Boals. "Expressive Writing Can Increase Working Memory Capacity." *Journal of Experimental Psychology* 130, no. 3 (2001): 520–533.

17. Andy Martens, Michael Johns, Jeff Greenberg, and Jeff Schimel. "Combating Stereotype Threat: The Effect of Self-Affirmation on Women's Intellectual Performance." *Journal of Experimental Social Psychology* 42, no. 2 (2006): 236–243.

18. Nurit Shnabel, Valerie Purdie-Vaughns, Jonathan E. Cook, Julio Garcia, and Geoffrey L. Cohen. "Demystifying Values-Affirmation Interventions: Writing About Social Belonging Is a Key to Buffering Against Identity Threat." *Personality and Social Psychology Bulletin* 39, no. 5 (March 10, 2013): 663–676.

19. Adam L. Alter, Joshua Aronson, John M. Darley, Cordaro Rodriguez, and Diane N. Ruble. "Rising to the Threat: Reducing Stereotype Threat by Reframing the Threat as a Challenge." *Journal of Experimental Social Psychology* 46, no. 1 (2010): 166–171.

20. Jeremy P. Jamieson, Wendy Berry Mendes, Erin Blackstock, and Toni Schmader. "Turning the Knots in Your Stomach into Bows: Reappraising Arousal Improves Performance on the GRE." *Journal of Experimental Social Psychology* 46, no. 1 (January 2010): 208–212.
21. Mark Leary. *Understanding the Mysteries of Human Behavior.* The Great Courses. (2013).
22. William Meek. "The Evolutionary Psychology of Anxiety." VeryWellMind. (November 18, 2019). Available at https://www.verywellmind.com/evolution-anxiety-1392983.
23. Fredric Neuman. "The Evolution of an Anxious Feeling." *Psychology Today.* (April 5, 2014). Available at https://www.psychologytoday.com/intl/blog/fighting-fear/201404/the-evolution-anxious-feeling.
24. Michigan Medicine, University of Michigan. "Stress Management: Breathing Exercises for Relaxation." (June 28, 2018). Available at https://www.uofmhealth.org/health-library/uz2255.
25. Harvard Health Publishing, Harvard Medical School. "Relaxation Techniques: Breath Control Helps Quell Errant Stress Response." (April 13, 2018). Available at https://www.health.harvard.edu/mind-and-mood/relaxation-techniques-breath-control-helps-quell-errant-stress-response.
26. Gurinder Singh Bains, Lee S. Berk, Noha Daher, Everett Lohman, Ernie Schwab, Jerrold Petrofsky, and Pooja Deshpande. "The Effect of Humor on Short-Term Memory in Older Adults: A New Component for Whole-Person Wellness." *Advances in Mind-Body Medicine* 28, no. 2 (March 2014): 16–24.

Section Four

1. Simply Hired. "Managers Reveal Their Practices and Opinions." (2018). Available at https://blog.simplyhired.com/hiring-truths/.

2. Jeffrey M. Conte and Rick R. Jacobs. "Validity Evidence Linking Polychronicity and Big Five Personality Dimensions to Absence, Lateness, and Supervisory Performance Ratings." *Human Performance* 16, no. 2 (2003): 107–129.

3. Jenny Shaw. "Punctuality and the Everyday Ethics of Time: Some Evidence from the Mass Observation Archive." *Time & Society* 3, no. 1 (February 1, 1994): 79–97.

4. Sumathi Reddy. "We Know Why You're Always Late." *Wall Street Journal.* (February 3, 2015).

5. David M. Sanbonmatsu, David L. Strayer, Nathan Medeiros-Ward, and Jason M. Watson. "Who Multi-Tasks and Why? Multi-Tasking Ability, Perceived Multi-Tasking Ability, Impulsivity, and Sensation Seeking." *PLoS ONE* 8, no. 1 (January 23, 2013): e54402.

6. Neils van de Ven, Leon van Rijswijk, and Michael M. Roy. "The Return Trip Effect: Why the Return Trip Often Seems to Take Less Time." *Psychonomic Bulletin & Review* 18, no. 5 (2011): 827–832.

7. Adoree Durayappah-Harrison. "The Real Reason Some of Us Are Chronically Late." *Psychology Today.* (November 14, 2014).

8. Simply Hired. "Managers Reveal Their Practices and Opinions." (2018). Available at https://blog.simplyhired.com/hiring-truths/.

9. Daniel Pink. *When: The Scientific Secrets of Perfect Timing.* Riverhead Books. (2018).

10. Daniel Pink. *When: The Scientific Secrets of Perfect Timing.* Riverhead Books. (2018).

11. Justin Caba. "Least Productive Time of the Day Officially Determined to Be 2:55 PM: What You Can Do to Stay Awake?" *Medical Daily.* (June 4, 2013).

12. MDedge. "How Much Sleep Is Required for Peak Cognitive Performance?" *Neurology Reviews.* (August 2015) Available at https://www.mdedge. com/neurology/article/101668/alzheimers-cognition/ how-much-sleep-required-peak-cognitive-performance.

13. Sumathi Reddy. "Why Seven Hours of Sleep Might Be Better Than Eight." *Wall Street Journal.* (July 21, 2014).

14. Laura Blue. "How Much Sleep Do You Really Need?" *Time.* (June 6, 2008).

15. Daniel A. Sternberg, Kacey Ballard, Joseph L. Hardy, Benjamin Katz, P. Murali Doraiswamy, and Michael Scanlon. "The Largest Human Cognitive Performance Dataset Reveals Insights Into the Effects of Lifestyle Factors and Aging." *Frontiers in Human Neuroscience 7,* no. 292 (June 20, 2013).

16. Jill Duffy. "Why Six Hours of Sleep Is as Bad as None at All." Fast Company. (March 7, 2016).

17. Alvin Powell. "Study Shows Importance of Sleep for Optimal Memory Functioning." *The Harvard Gazette.* (February 15, 2007).

18. National Sleep Foundation. "How Lack of Sleep Impacts Cognitive Performance and Focus." Available at https://www.sleepfoundation.org/articles/ how-lack-sleep-impacts-cognitive-performance-and-focus.

19. Harvard Medical School, Division of Sleep Medicine. "Twelve Simple Tips to Improve Your Sleep." (December 18, 2007). Available at http://healthysleep.med.harvard. edu/healthy/getting/overcoming/tips.

20. Centre for Clinical Interventions. "Sleep Hygiene." Available at https://www.cci.health.wa.gov.au/~/media/cci/mental%20health%20professionals/sleep/sleep%20-%20information%20sheets/sleep%20information%20sheet%20-%2004%20-%20sleep%20hygiene.pdf.

21. Centers for Disease Control and Prevention. "Tips for Better Sleep." (July 15, 2016). Available at https://www.cdc.gov/sleep/about_sleep/sleep_hygiene.html.

22. Shona L. Halson. "Sleep and the Elite Athlete." Gatorade Sports Science Institute. (May 2013). Available at https://www.gssiweb.org/sports-science-exchange/article/sse-113-sleep-and-the-elite-athlete.

23. S. Beagrie. "If You Only Do Five Things . . ." *Personnel Today.* (September 23, 2003): 29.

24. Patti Shank. "Science of Learning 101: What Kind of Practice Makes Expert?" Association for Talent Development. (May 26, 2016). Available at https://www.td.org/insights/science-of-learning-101-what-kind-of-practice-makes-expert.

25. Annie Bosler and Don Greene. "How to Practice Effectively . . . For Just About Anything." TEDEd. Available at https://ed.ted.com/lessons/how-to-practice-effectively-for-just-about-anything-annie-bosler-and-don-greene.

Landing A Job During A Crisis: The New Abnormal

1. Holly Secon, Aylin Woodward and Dave Mosher. "A Comprehensive Timeline of the New Coronavirus Pandemic, From China's First COVID-19 Case to the Present." Business Insider. (April 23, 2020)

2. OWL Labs. "State of Remote Work." Available at https://www.owllabs.com/state-of-remote-work

Phone and Video Interviews: The New Normal

1. Maddie Shepherd. "28 Surprising Working From Home Statistics." Fundera. (April 7, 2020). Available at https://www.fundera.com/resources/working-from-home-statistics
2. Jonathan I. Dingel and Brent Neiman. "How Many Jobs Can be Done at Home?" Becker Friedman Institute for Economics. (April 16, 2020). Available at https://bfi.uchicago.edu/wp-content/uploads/BFI_White-Paper_Dingel_Neiman_3.2020.pdf
3. Global Workplace Analytics. "How Many People Could Work-From-Home." Available at https://globalworkplaceanalytics.com/how-many-people-could-work-from-home
4. Global Workplace Analytics. "Work-At-Home After Covid-19—Our Forecast." Available at https://globalworkplaceanalytics.com/work-at-home-after-covid-19-our-forecast
5. Gonz Sánchez. "2019 Hiring Statistics, Trends & Data: The Ultimate List of Recruitment Stats." Jobbatical. Available at https://jobbatical.com/resources/hiring-statistics
6. Michael W. Kraus. "Voice-only Communication Enhances Empathic Accuracy." *American Psychologist* 72, no. 7 (2017): 644–654.
7. Tara L. Kraft and Sarah D. Pressman. "Grin and Bear It: The Influence of Manipulated Facial Expression on the Stress Response." *Psychological Science* 23, no. 11 (September 24, 2012): 1372-1378.
8. Nicholas A. Coles, Jeff T. Larsen, and Heather C. Lench. "A Meta-analysis of the Facial Feedback Literature." *Psychological Bulletin* 145, no. 6 (2019): 610–651
9. Madeleine A. Fugère. "Why Seeing Photos of Ourselves Disappoints Us." *Psychology Today.* (October 10, 2017). Available at https://www.psychologytoday.com/us/blog/dating-and-mating/201710/why-seeing-photos-ourselves-disappoints-us.

www.ingramcontent.com/pod-product-compliance
Lightning Source LLC
Chambersburg PA
CBHW070804050426
42452CB00011B/1888